’TwixT

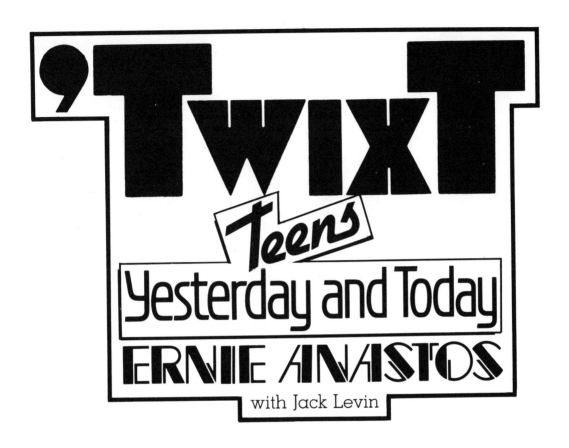

'TWIXT

Teens

Yesterday and Today

ERNIE ANASTOS

with Jack Levin

A GROLIER COMPANY

Franklin Watts
New York | London | Toronto
Sydney

1983

Library of Congress Cataloging in Publication Data:

Anastos, Ernie.
    'Twixt, teens yesterday and today.

    1. Youth—United States—History—20th century.
I. Levin, Jack, 1941–   . II. Title.
HQ796.A683   1983   305.2′3′0973   83-3655
ISBN 0-531-09890-7
ISBN 0-531-09953-9 (pbk.)

To those young people around the world who for social, economic, political, or other reasons have been denied the opportunity to be teenagers.

Acknowledgments

'Twixt celebrates the American teenager. We as authors wish to celebrate in turn those individuals who so graciously shared their expertise and the institutions that shared the resources with us. We are deeply grateful for the assistance of numerous authorities, advisers, collectors, institutions, news and information organizations, museums, schools and universities, and historical societies who participated in all aspects of this project. We are especially thankful to those wonderful people across the country who so generously related their memories and personal recollections of teenage life in America. We have profited greatly from their help, enthusiasm, and hospitality. This book would have been impossible without their efforts.

Our heartfelt thanks to the School of Education, Harvard University; Low Library, Columbia University; Alice Ilchman, President, Sarah Lawrence College; Midge Turk Richardson, *Seventeen* magazine; Nat Andriani, United Press International; Ev Arnold, Josten Yearbook Division; Stavros Cosmopulos, Cosmopulos, Crowley & Daly, Inc.; Jack Haber, *Gentleman's Quarterly*; Fashion Institute of Technology; John Durniak, *The New York Times*; David Hume Kennerly, Time, Inc.; Automobile Information Council; Al Burns, *Car Dealer Inside Newsletter*; Peter Christopoulos, Time-Life, Inc.; George Gallup, Jr., The Gallup Organization; Drake-Chenault Enterprises; Norm N. Nite, WCBS-FM; and the New York Public Library Schomberg Center for Research in Black Culture.

We are also grateful to the Smithsonian Institution; Mel Phillips, CBS International Records; James Brady, *New York Post*; Library of Congress; Bureau of Indian Affairs, Washington, D.C.; George Maksian, *New York Daily News*; Pam Kerr, Time-Life, Inc.; the staff at Larchmont Public Library, Larchmont, New York; the staff at Sharon Public Library, Sharon, Massachusetts; Chinese Cultural Foundation, San Francisco; Lynne Ames, *The New York Times*; Rye Country Day School, Rye, New York; Janine Linden, Compton Advertising; Ruth Mann, Chapel Hill-Chauncey Hall School; The

Associated Press; *Billboard* magazine; New York's 92nd Street YMYW Hebrew Association; and to Roger Allan, Dick Corbin, and the late Chris Nikitas for their encouragement.

We very much appreciate the assistance of Lila Leibowitz and Ron McAllister of the Department of Sociology and Anthropology, and Research Librarian Andrew Calo of Northeastern University, Boston, Massachusetts. And we extend thanks to our dedicated research staff—Ginny Lederberger, Esther Pessin, Lois Katz, Joanne Kritikos, and Rhonda Paradis, Charles Varanas and other students at Northeastern University—for their hard work and energy.

To Elizabeth Hock, our editor, a special word of gratitude. Her insight and guidance were invaluable. We thank Liz for making important recommendations regarding our manuscript and appreciate her dedication. We also thank our book designer, Jackie Schuman, our picture researcher, Yvonne Gerin, and our literary agent, Sally Wecksler.

Finally, we are indebted to our families, whose ardent support and patience through long months of research, travel, and writing cannot be measured. To Kelly, Nina, and Phillip Anastos, and to Flea, Michael, Bonnie, and Andrea Levin, kisses.

Contents

A Special Foreword
by Robert F. Kennedy, Jr.

My father and my uncle, President Kennedy, believed the fundamental resource of this nation to be its young people. They looked to youth not just for the Peace Corps, not just for the civil rights movement, but as the hope for a better future.

One of my father's legacies to me was a volume of Tennyson's poems. While my father was apt to scribble and doodle in the books he liked most, the Tennyson contains just one underlined passage. Knowing his fatalism, his prescience, and his fear that his children would grow up without him, I believe he may have marked this passage from "Ulysses" for us, his children, and for future generations.

> Come, my friends,
> 'Tis not too late to seek a newer world.
> Push off, and sitting well in order smite
> The sounding furrows; for my purpose holds
> To sail beyond the sunset, and the baths
> Of all the western stars, until I die.
> It may be that the gulfs will wash us down;
> It may be we shall touch the Happy Isles,
> And see the great Achilles, whom we
>   knew.
> Though much is taken, much abides; and
>   though
> We are not now that strength which in old
>   days
> Moved earth and heaven, that which we
>   are, we are;
> One equal temper of heroic hearts,
> Made weak by time and fate, but strong in
>   will
> To strive, to seek, to find, and not to yield.

A Foreword by
Brooke Shields

I believe that the teen years are a special time in one's life, a time I know I'd never want to miss.

I am fortunate to receive letters from teenagers all over the country who express personal feelings about their lives and the world around them. They tell me they care about what happens to them—to their bodies and their minds. They are concerned not only for themselves but for future generations as well. They seek to build a better world by forging stronger ties with their families and their friends—the kinds of relationships which are bound to affect their work, their marriages, and their lifestyles in a positive way.

This book is probably long overdue, but it's never too late to celebrate America's teenagers.

Introduction

I remember my youth and the feeling that it will never come back any more—the feeling that I could last forever...
                                                              Joseph Conrad

'Twixt is a celebration of America's teenagers, a tribute to those "between" years—'twixt years!

We all have our memories of those years, many of which lie moldering somewhere with the tassel from the mortarboard, the yearbooks, the diaries with tiny keys long lost, the yellowed clippings, and faded photographs. And then there are the memories that have never really been put away, that rush forth at the first bar of that special song, at the ring of an old expression, at a whiff of a long-forgotten fragrance. It is all of these—and more—that we hope to unlock with 'Twixt.

How easy it once was to scoff at adults who, with a wisdom we could not appreciate, said, "This is the best time of your life. Enjoy it." Or, "Someday you'll wish you were eighteen again." We think they were right.

We feel the teen years are a history worth preserving. American teenagers have always had an unparalleled opportunity for self-expression. They have affected social and political attitudes, and have had a dramatic impact on our fashions, fads, dance steps, hairstyles, and even speech.

It wasn't always so. In the 1920s the rapid influx of young people from the labor force into the schools sparked a phenomenon in American society; by the late 1930s this unique subculture was firmly enough established to be given a name all its own: teenager.

'Twixt is the result of a long desire on our part to do a book that focused on the positive aspects of the teen years. At the age of sixteen I hosted my first radio program, the purpose of which was to interview teenagers on a wide range of subjects—from politics to dating. Later, as a news reporter and television anchorman, I produced a series of programs on youth in various parts of the country, all the while collecting and assembling information toward the day when my dream of a book and a television documentary on teens would be realized. Jack Levin, under whom I studied sociology at Northeastern University in Boston, Massachusetts, and who has conducted numerous studies on youth and who regularly addresses groups of young people and their parents on a variety of subjects, shared my enthusiasm.

In 'Twixt we have endeavored not to compile a catalog of catalogs nor a book of lists of twentieth-century teens but to present a historical and pictorial essay, a brief yearbook of the teen years from 1920 to 1983.

Each generation of teens has forged its own style, from Flaming Youth of the twenties to punk 'n' preppie of the eighties. 'Twixt is our toast to them all—wild, crazy, starry-eyed, stubborn, sincere, impulsive, vulnerable, restless, impressionable—to that part of our lives that can never be relived, that should never be forgotten.

'TwixT

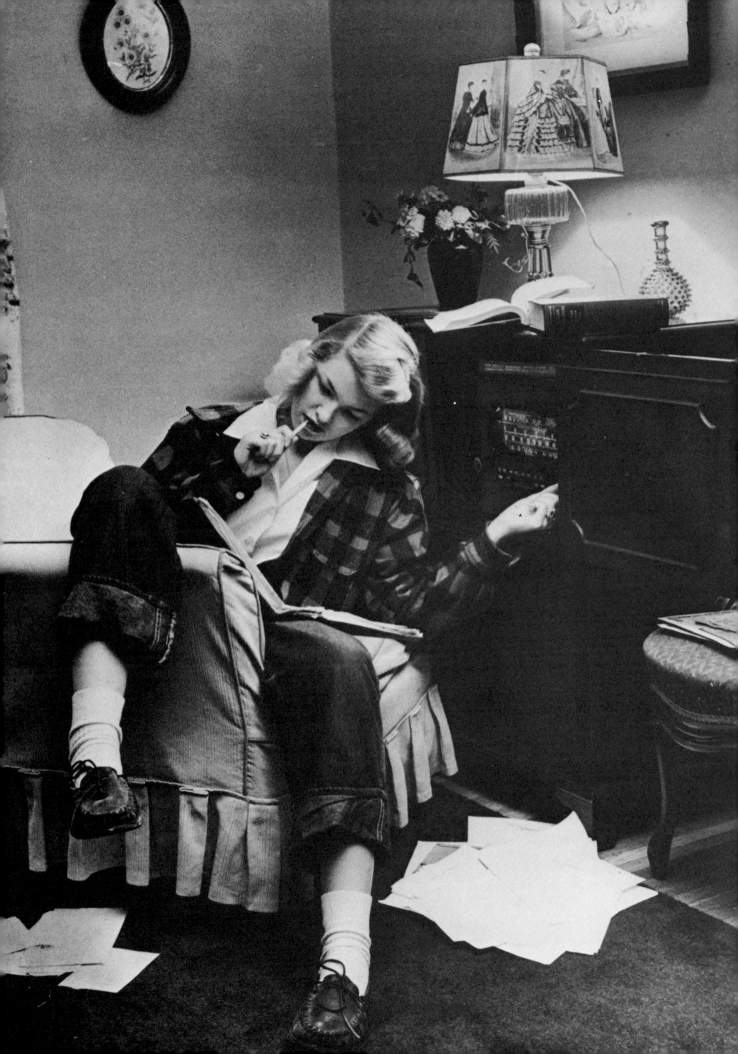

See You After Class

I graduated from high school, and in my day *that* was a sizeable accomplishment. I was proud! *(1927)*
                                            Dolores H., Illinois

My father took French in school. I'm learning to speak Apple! *(1983)*   *David M., Massachusetts*

8:15. The bell rings. Suddenly halls are jammed, voices collide ("I forgot my homework!" "There's a *test* today?"), lockers clang, books are juggled, notes are hastily passed, and the race for homeroom is on. Another day at Your Town·High School!

School is where so much of it happened—where we lived, laughed, cried, and maybe learned something. But it wasn't always that way.

Until the twentieth century, adolescence was rarely regarded as a distinct period in one's life. A young person went to work as soon as he or she was able, even if it meant staying away from school. Around 1920, however, the situation changed dramatically. The industrialization of America and increased prosperity, compulsory education and child labor laws, and a rapidly swelling immigrant work force freed young people past the age of puberty to go to school full time; before long, high-school enrollments swelled to nearly five million.

Overnight the twenties became the decade of the young. Having a good time was paramount, worrying about the future was unthinkable. Mad, bad, glad, the Jazz Age, the Flaming Twenties, and the Era of Excess describe the decade aptly. Despite the fact that the most popular phrase was "back to normalcy," social change happened at breakneck speed.

The mood in the high schools was almost as buoyant as that on college campuses across the land. The twenties were, after all, the golden age of Joe College. Big-time sports, especially football, a freer attitude toward the opposite sex, and more open and widespread use of alcohol proved powerful influences for all those high-school students who could actually entertain the prospect of going to college, such was the prosperity of the times.

The curriculum ran to the standard and traditional, but extracurricular activities such as clubs and sports expanded rapidly and were attended with gusto.

The thirties saw the nation crippled by the Great Depres-

"I didn't mind it, but I had to help all my brothers go to college. I worked. *(1928)*
    Jayne F., Massachusetts

We didn't have the educational opportunities. Anyone who grew up in the twenties knows it was a big deal if you finished high school. *(1920)*
    Nora C., New York

We respected our teachers. They were no different from ministers or priests. They had that kind of image. *(1928)*
    John W., New York

1916

sion and a number of teenagers dropped out of school to help their families. Surprisingly, the decade was a particularly wonderful time to be in high school—so much so that those years were frequently remembered as "the golden years." The high school took its place as the focal point for teens. Sports and other school activities flowered as never before; students flocked to join peace clubs, rifle clubs, public-speaking groups, theater societies, and school newspaper staffs. The mood was so buoyant that many a high-school corridor rang with lusty renditions of "Down in the Meadow in the Itty Bitty Poo!"

If the late thirties were the best possible time to be in high school, the early forties witnessed a change in focus for teens. Most had at least one family member, boyfriend, or neighbor who was in uniform. The war quickly found its way into the nation's high schools, and the clubs of the thirties gave way to various war efforts where teens knitted socks for GIs and wrote letters and sent packages to them. The traditional curriculum underwent subtle but lasting changes, too. The emphasis was now on citizenship training, and teens found themselves studying problems of democracy.

As high-school enrollments climbed in the forties and fifties, the age at which one reached puberty appeared to

School was fun. I was happy wearing Levi's overalls . . . listening to the Lone Ranger on the radio and going roller skating. We called skates "gayblades." *(1931)*
Lena S., Vermont

They didn't encourage us to play sports in those days. My mother thought it was too masculine. They just didn't think it was good for a girl. *(1931)*
Edith K., Delaware

SEE YOU AFTER CLASS

5

1920s

There'll be a short quiz on Friday...

1943

1916

1930

I don't know how I would have made it through high school if my parents hadn't helped me with homework—every kid must have done that. *(1941)*
Dot G., Arkansas

fall. While wild parties, dating, and dances generally remained the province of high-school teens, such was the appeal of being a teenager that much of their life-style filtered down to the elementary schools where sixth graders, ever anxious to imitate their older brothers and sisters, seized upon the special slang, fashions—and cigarettes.

The word *teenager* may date from the thirties, but the indelible image of the American teenager is the one that emerged full blown—ponytailed, d.a.'ed, leather-jacketed, letter-sweatered, poodle-skirted, and bobby-soxed—in the fifties. Now the corridors rang with good-natured jibes between Joe College and greaser, and the bustle moved beyond

1931

1970s

school walls to the rapidly expanding parking lots, home to an incomparable array of teen machines—cars!

Power mechanics—or auto shop—supplanted wood shop and metal shop, but the traditional high-school activities remained strong as ever: student council, yearbook, assemblies, proms, and football games—although the last two undoubtedly generated the lion's share of excitement and attention.

A word about the high-school yearbook. Those madras-covered annuals have been around for a long time (although they appear to be in danger of being displaced by the multimedia version of the eighties, which includes a cassette, a nonbook of freestanding display cards, and button pins!). The picture taking, ordering, and signing rituals have always been an important part of those 'twixt years. Personal notes from teachers and principals were a touch of status, as were chummy messages from beauty queens, Student Council presidents, cheerleaders, and athletes. Most teens busily reserved blank pages and certain pictures for special friends. (It was, of course, a given that you hated your own picture.) But no matter how carefully you set up a memorable yearbook, there was always some clod who signed on your steady's page, or a yearbook staffer who saw to it that *your* name appeared under the picture of the school janitor. Perhaps the most fun of all is returning to those pages years later to see what your old steady—or husband or wife or secret heartthrob—wrote.

By the mid-1960s, tradition had virtually become a dirty word. Teens still screamed and yelled on the school bus, but they also did it in class. "Cool" meant never playing a sport or attending a game! School officials may have required girls to kneel on the floor to determine if skirts were the proper length, but in general students had more options and greater freedom than ever before.

Open classrooms, modular systems, and alternative education were considered a great leap in the direction of a more relaxed atmosphere for learning. Accordingly, dress codes were jettisoned in favor of "anything goes"; boys were encouraged to take home economics as girls enrolled in the shop courses; co-ed gym classes were not uncommon; and the good old proms were regularly abandoned in favor of keg parties. But unlike those *Happy Days* prosperous fifties,

I used to write notes to my girlfriend in school all the time. We'd meet in the hallway between classes and exchange them. That was the best part about school for me. *(1959)*
Bill F., Nebraska

There was always someone who carried a bologna sandwich around or left one in their desk, stinking up the whole room. It made some people hungry; it made me sick! *(1956)*
Paul V., Louisiana

I was really ugly, like the ugliest kid in the school. I was so self-conscious about it—never dared to ask a girl out. To add to the problem, I wasn't very good at sports. I remember wishing that I could play something—anything. *(1964)*		*Tony S., Ohio*

the even greater prosperity of the sixties was offset by the constant rumble of distant thunder which teens could not wholly ignore: race riots, the death of a president, the Vietnam War, and campus unrest. Yet the good times in high school were still to be had, and worrying about the future continued to be taboo, as the "jam today" attitude reached epic proportions.

It didn't last. By the mid-seventies, parents, teachers, and administrators were calling for a return to order, discipline, and high standards. Somewhere along the road to alternative schooling, learning had fallen way behind—with disastrous results; now it was imperative that the core curriculum and basic skills of old be stressed again, but the approach was fresh.

"Retro" described a lot more than studies by the late seventies and early eighties. Teens passed over the informal, no-rules clothing in favor of updated classics and—surprise!—flashy, *forties* and *fifties* garb. Preppie mingled easily enough with punk and new wave, and the halls rang again with talk of college and dances.

The school bus was a zoo. There was so much yelling going on—there was no way you could study for a test! *(1968)*
Charles B., Connecticut

1941

1957

I'd hold hands with my girlfriend in school. She'd get so darn nervous about it. But I wasn't worried—we sat in the back row in the corner. *(1963) Hank C., Massachusetts*

1953

1957

What is significant about high school in the eighties is the importance of and interest in sports on the part of virtually everyone—not just jocks. The legacy of the seventies—where an increased awareness of an unhealthy environment, a near obsession with physical fitness, and Eat Right to Live Right were writ large—is a commitment to a healthy way of life, and one which teens have eagerly embraced. While soccer, rugby, and aerobic dancing have broadened the standard sports offerings, jogging, the sport available to anyone willing to put on a pair of sneaks and run, has lured more teens than ever before into physical activity.

When I ask myself what I want to be when I grow up—the answer is simple. I want to stay a teenager—I love it. *(1982)*
Ronnie H., Texas

Let's face it. The various decades have stamped the high-school experience variously, but the basics never really change. High school is still the place where a teenager spends most of his or her day, where Student Councils, yearbooks, assemblies, proms, clubs, detentions, sports, and just plain getting together color those days, and from where some of our fondest memories spring.

I was always wanting to be older. But when I hit twenty-one—I wanted to stop there and be seventeen again. *(1948)*
Harriet B., Indiana

We all kept talking about graduation so much. I don't know why we'd get so excited, because when it finally came we were feeling terrible. It felt like I had lost my mother or something, if you can believe that. *(1955)*
Daphne P., Pennsylvania

1929

Some day it *will* be over!

1920s

1943

1980s

1970s

I never let schooling interfere with
my education. *Mark Twain*

1980s

1980s

1970s

2 Wheels

On Saturday, I'd practically spend the whole day just waxing and cleaning up my '49 DeSoto—getting it ready for my date. I even remember spraying the inside with after-shave lotion; you know, it felt more like an apartment than my car. Oh, yes, and I'd always ask my mother for a few extra bucks for gas! *(1960)*

Alex A., New Hampshire

Teenagers and cars— an ongoing love affair since the first Model T rolled out in 1908. Henry Ford himself talked about his "Tin Lizzie" with great affection, even though it was the subject of endless jokes, tall tales, and ridicule. Nevertheless, his marvelous invention rapidly changed America.

The Roaring Twenties were the golden age of motoring. Billions of dollars were spent to maintain and improve the nation's highways. For the first time, a majority of American families owned a car. By 1929, the competition within the auto industry was fierce, resulting in a wide variety of automobiles and prices; Ford coupe, $350; Nash Whippet, $495; Studebaker Erskine-Six, $995; and Cadillac's V-8, $2500. Other popular cars included the Maxwell, Buick, Reo, Auburn, Oldsmobile, Willys, and Franklin. In fact, there were at least fifty American-made autos! Nearly five million cars were being sold yearly. By the end of the decade, total motor vehicle registrations were close to twenty-two million. The country was rolling along on four wheels!

It wasn't long before young people latched onto cars as something *made* for them. Cars represented freedom, independence, privacy, status, and popularity. College students dubbed one special breed "jalopies"—bumperless cars that ran without a starter, temp gauge, or even a speedometer. It didn't matter at all; cars were meant to be fun! If you had one, it could belong to everyone. Friends would pile in, pitch in for gas, and roar off on a merry mission.

Through the thirties, young drivers drove jauntily around town and campus, jazzing up football games with their brightly colored "freak cars," whose hoods and doors were plastered with favorite expressions—like "loose." Rah-rah!

By the 1940s the automobile had firmly established itself as an object of fascination for teens. More than a conveyance, it was now a place to *go*—especially for dates. A car was an "apartment on wheels" where young people could neck and pet. Suddenly, the formalities that had constrained their parents—like curfews and chaperones—evaporated. The car

My friend Mike owned a Ford, a Model T. They used to call it a flivver. So we'd ride around after school and sing this song to see how many girls would notice: 'It's a rambling flivver, a rambling flivver. Step on her tail and then stay with her.' Boy, that was fun—and crazy! *(1927)*
Matt J., Montana

I had a real noisy, beat up Model T when I was in school. I called it a Rolls-Rough. *(1931)*
Peter K., Alabama

I remember freak cars were plastered with writing and designs. It was a big deal to ride around in them with a bunch of guys. *(1947)*
Paul V., California

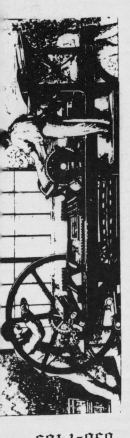

Village Shopping Cent[er]
Lake Oswego

Tis the good Reader that makes the good Book   Emerson

The Book Cellar
636-7403

1928

1940

I did homework, listened to the radio, ate—even slept!—in my car. Best $200 I ever spent. *(1949)* *Frank B., Missouri*

1958

Teenagers and cars—
an ongoing love affair.

1958

1960s

1981

1970s

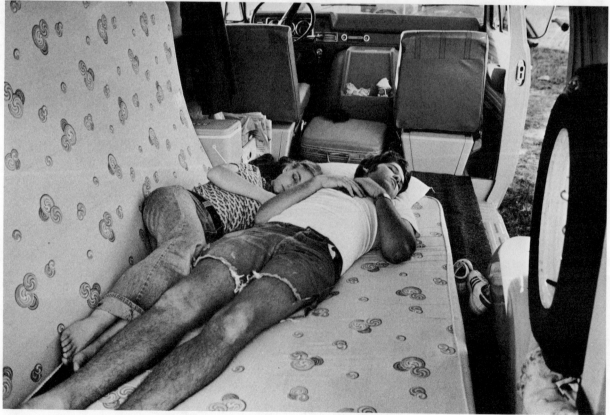

1970s

'TWIXT

had helped to change the whole dating, rating, and mating game!

There is no question that the car was rapidly transforming the middle-class American life-style and the American landscape. It spawned highways, gas stations, roadside diners, motels, billboards, and suburbs. After the war, the economic upswing changed the nation's buying power dramatically. Even teenagers could buy cars! By 1950 fifty-four million cars were on the road, more than double the number at the end of World War II. Teens, who primarily purchased used cars, were now a very distinct market—not to mention audience—and one the auto industry could not ignore.

Automobiles quickly became not only affordable but more colorful, comfortable, and powerful. In 1955 a record 7.9 million new cars were sold, and nearly 16 million used cars rolled into America's driveways.

Teenagers, ever inventive, brought their talents to bear on ways to use and dress up their cars. During the fifties, they crowded into the parking lots of drive-in restaurants and

We'd all pitch in for gas and go to the beach or wherever. This was the best part of being a teenager, being together in a car. *(1941)*
Brad P., Pennsylvania

My friend drove a 1934 Plymouth. He called it the Plymouth Rock and said, 'Anyone who steps in better come across!' *(1946)*
Stan K., New York

1969

Apartments on wheels.

carhop joints, took their dates to drive-in movies, and turned up the old radio and cruised the streets of town—the better to pick up a date or find a party! In small towns, particularly in the West, this cruising was virtually the only entertainment; endless lines of cars filled with teens who flirted and/or cat-called with each other streamed relentlessly up and down the main drag—as was emphatically portrayed in the movie *American Graffiti*.

Everything appeared to revolve around one's having a car. It was *the* place to hang out, drink beer, take a nap, study, make out, impress the girls, and drag-race. Before the big football games, it was often *de rigueur* for high-school students to parade their crepe-paper-bedecked, banner-laden cars through town, blowing horns and shouting cheers at the top of their lungs.

For the Joe College Ivy League types, the Corvette was the car of choice, though some were known to prefer an MG roadster with dish wheels. But for many fifties boys, the '49 Ford or Mercury was the car to make their own wheels spin—especially if it had skirts, dual exhaust, lowered back, primer paint job, and dice hanging from the rearview mirror! Cars and hot rods provided teens with an ongoing work project, and no amount of tinkering ever was too much; this was purely and simply a labor of love.

It was in the West that the car *culture* began to boom in 1963. Not since the '51 Ford with mud flaps and a raccoon tail on the aerial had the automobile been so important. With virtually no public transportation to speak of in the West, a car was such a necessity that teens commonly had their own and were not dependent on the family station wagon. Cars were a way of life, an essential rather than a convenience or luxury.

The sixties saw all kinds of options become available— vinyl roofs, FM stereo, automatic transmission, power brakes and steering, power windows, and Powerglide. But the 1955, '56, and '57 Chevy Hardtop were still the teens' favorites— those two-door sedans slicked up with mags or chrome wheels, oversized tires, and a taxicab-yellow paint job.

Why only a flashy new Corvette or XKE could compete! Boys spoke in tongues—overhead cams, fuel injection, turbines. For girls, the situation was clear: Love me, love my car—especially the hum of a well-tuned engine. Girls learned

There are wheels—
and there are wheels.

1979

1981

1940

1949

1957

1960s

1956

My Chevy van was far out. I spent a fortune
decorating it. *(1972) George V., Ohio*

When I was fourteen I began dreaming (praying, actually) that I would get a red, 1952 MG with wire wheels for my sixteenth birthday. I spent an awful lot of time imagining myself driving around in one, turning heads— it was very sexy. *(1961)*
Elizabeth H., Connecticut

My brother drove a car to school. When I got to high school it was a bike! *(1975)*
Lewis H., Delaware

My father asks me where I went with the car last night and I say, 'Just riding around.' He takes one look at the speedometer and yells, 'Seventy-five miles *worth?*' *(1982)*   *Dan C., Rhode Island*

a lot about forbearance, too; a significant number of picnics and movies were regularly passed over in favor of an outing to the local drag strip.

Songwriters churned out hit tunes about the wonders of the highways and those little deuce coupes. The Hondells, Ronny and the Daytonas, Jan and Dean, and most of all, the Beach Boys sang odes to their Hondas, GTOs, and T-Birds, not to mention Dead Man's Curve and the Little Old Lady from Pasadena!

The sixties also welcomed in droves of European imports, many of which were affordable to young drivers—or their parents. The most familiar colored dot on the landscape, of course, was the Volkswagen "bug." High-school parking lots, in fact, became so "international" that a guest lecturer at an Eastern high school in 1964 was moved to comment that the students must have to assume the fetal position in order to drive! But the most significant change in the youth car culture arrived in the mid- to late sixties when the half-ton pickup and van chugged onto the scene and became instant successes. West Coast kids, accustomed to toting their surfing gear in the legendary "woodies," now carted their stuff around with ease; not since the Nash Rambler had any vehicle provided such leg room! The van quickly earned its name as the sin bin.

Social changes, specifically women's rights, affected the teen car culture. For the first time, more girls were buying cars and were not relying upon boyfriends or family to supply them with wheels.

Teenagers' love affair with the automobile continued on into the seventies and eighties, but there were some rude awakenings. The energy crisis and inflation slowed the stream of acquisitions considerably. Fuel-efficient, four-cylinder models like the Datsun, Toyota, Pinto, Honda, and Chevette replaced the souped-up gas-eater V-8s of the fifties and the tony sports cars of the sixties and early seventies. Gone, too, were the more affordable jalopies of the past. Used-car prices and insurance rates climbed skyward together. Parents were pressed into helping shoulder the car payments, and teen car buying slipped conspicuously.

The trusty family car, however, is still around and may just reclaim its place as the primary set of teen wheels, but it is doubtful that the car will ever again be *the* focal point of the teen life-style. Alas.

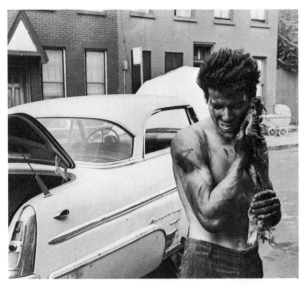

1950s

1958

1980s

Having a car is excellent. All your friends pitch
in for gas. It's about the only way you can make
it—if everyone pitches in! *(1983) Dean W., California*

Won't You Wear My Ring?

The difficult thing about making out was this. You had to slooowly get your arm around her, then let it drop on her shoulder eeeasy. My heart would pound while I was doing that and waiting to see what she would do. *(1937)* *Nick P., Wyoming*

Summers were great. I'd always have a song that would remind me of some guy. It would like build up all summer, and to this day it still reminds me of him. *(1961)* *Allison B., Connecticut*

A survey in a Midwestern city turned up some interesting things about teenagers. Many high-school students told the interviewers that they argue with their parents about the number of times they are permitted to go out on school nights, about the hour they are expected to get home, about the use of the family car, and about spending money. A number of them also reported going to at least one sex party during their high-school years.

Not surprising, you say? Perhaps, but you should also know that the survey was conducted January 1924!

Smoking, drinking, all-night car rides. The adolescent antics of twenties' teens were probably somewhat tame by today's standards, but not by comparison with their own middle-class standards. The gap separating Flaming Youth from their elders appears to have been just as wide as it is today. In 1924, however, it seemed that every standard of decency was being destroyed by members of the younger generation. Drunkenness was commonplace at proms, big football games, and house-party weekends. College administrators responded to on-campus "cheek-to-cheek dancing" and "unnecessary cuddling" by banning them.

The flappers shocked the country by smoking and drinking in public. By mid-decade, however, the cigarette had been accepted even by "nice" women of all ages, who smoked at parties, on trains, in theater lobbies, and in restaurants—though not in school.

Teenage partygoers delighted at the game of Murders (supervised, if you please, by adults) where a couple would hide in a closet and neck until the "murderer" was found! Even more popular were the petting parties of the early twenties. Alas, there was no lack of gossip about young, unmarried women from "nice" families who had spent lost weekends with men and who might even confess previous exploits to prospective husbands. Chastity and fidelity had gone the way of a lot of other things, to be sure, but young people refrained from broadcasting their experiences.

I didn't have any money to spend on a date. We'd go out, in a group most of the time. We were scared stiff to get into any trouble with a girl, but we never knew that much about sex anyway. *(1921)*
Joe H., Rhode Island

Don't kid yourself. There was just as much going on in my day as there is now. It just wasn't talked about or publicized. *(1928)*
Mason M., Arkansas

'TWIXT

1960s

1950s

Away from the spying eyes of parents.

1963

CALDWELL BRANCH
THE IDAHO
FIRST NATIONAL
BANK
ESTABLISHED 1867

1941

1964

1940s

1981

I remember going to the movies and then for a soda with my girl, Andrea. The whole date cost about twenty-five cents! *(1931)* *Leonard H., New York*

I didn't have a car, so we'd smooch in the backyard. *(1940)* *Jerry K., Indiana*

If a girl was kind of weird-looking, we'd call her scuzzy—but if she was really cute, she was a moose. See if anyone remembers that one! *(1945)* *Bernard H., New York*

With the onset of the Great Depression, a lot of those twenties' luxuries disappeared. For teens of the Swing generation, dating was frequently a cooperative affair; a girls' clique and a boys' clique got together at a party, picnic, dance, or hayride, and couples paired off for the evening. Or, a group of boys might make the rounds of several girls' homes, and the group would go on to a movie. During the thirties and forties less than one in five high-school students dated a person on a steady basis.

The vast majority of teenagers preferred "playing the field," but they *did* have sex on their minds. As early as 1936, a study of students at forty-six colleges and universities found that half of the men and one-quarter of the women had had premarital sex.

For Depression-era teens, cars were few and far between—and tended to be driven by girls, who were considered more trustworthy! Liquor all but disappeared from teen parties, but every class had a couple of boys who were known to overindulge occasionally, then show up in school bleary-eyed after their 'binge-y."

The drugstore and local soda shop were both hangout and dance floor, especially after school, when the favorite afternoon snack was a black-and-white shake with a side order of jelly doughnuts!

The forties saw the Saturday-night dance become as much a part of a teenager's life as saddle shoes. Sponsored by clubs, schools, and local ballrooms, these dances featured a bouncy teen band and eats like soft drinks and finger sandwiches. Depending on the mood of the dancers, the music was either "hot" or "sweet."

For girls, the slumber party presented a viable and fun-filled alternative to the Saturday-night date. Sporting their fathers' oversized pajamas and heads full of pin curls, they munched on their favorite yummies—popcorn and Moxie—and talked and giggled about boys into the wee hours before squeezing themselves into a couple of beds for an even smaller bit of shut-eye.

Making "love chains" (also called idiot chains) by linking folded chewing-gum wrappers was the number one make-him-love-me fad since the invention of the wishing well. A girl made a chain as long as her boyfriend was tall, burned it, and left the ashes to ensure a long, happy romance. Some

It was different dating in the forties. Guys had respect for their dates—they had to. And we left a lot to the imagination. *(1942) Andrew L., Utah*

1944

1947

girls even gave the chain to the boy, then got it back to burn when they broke up.

"Going steady," one of the many legacies of the fifties, indicated an exclusive relationship between boy and girl—at *least* for a few weeks! Often the relationship was announced to the world by the exchange of identification bracelets, scarves, school letters, parkas, rings, or wearing a fraternity pin (an event accorded an elaborate ceremony on many campuses). A girl might wear her steady's ring on a chain around her neck, but many opted for the more obvious display on the hand, which usually required that the back of the ring be wrapped tightly with colored string or yarn which was then painted with clear nail polish. A bona fide ring guard was the "ultimate utmost!"

Going steady may have helped relieve the anxiety about dating for teenagers of the fifties, but it usually increased it for their parents who suspected that so much contact with the same person must inevitably lead to "going all the way."

Like their counterparts in the preceding decades, teenage boys continued to divide the female population into two groups: *nice* girls to respect and admire, and *bad* girls to have fun with. The double standard permitted men to vent their "stronger" urges and judged women harshly for engaging in sex before marriage. Sociologist James Coleman has suggested that some teenage boys of the fifties developed a different rating system: *active* girls to respect *and* have a good time with, and *passive* girls to ignore. This distinction was particularly obvious to those who went steady and therefore professed absolute respect for one another. Thus, what was disapproved in a dating relationship became perfectly acceptable between teens who went steady; they could neck, pet, and maybe even "do it."

On the lighter side, fifties teens moved in a world that virtually catered to them. Cars, those veritable apartments on wheels, opened up their world; drive-in theaters and drive-in restaurants were made for teens with wheels. And the wheels made another big difference: a place *away* from the spying eyes of parents! The "post office" kissing games were no longer confined to closets and dark corners at parties; the privacy of the car ensured that a lot more than kissing could continue uninterrupted.

The local malt shop and pizza parlor—presided over by

perpetually *warm* jukeboxes—were the favorite homes away from homes for hordes of Archies, Veronicas, Reggies, Bettys, and yes, even Jugheads. From those pregame gatherings where you went to find a ride, eye anyone you had a crush on, and maybe, just maybe, flirt a little; to postgame revelry with the team, where the possibility of *still* finding a Saturday-night date charged the carousing with another kind of spark; to the after-the-dance (or -movies or -party) required appearance, those pine-paneled walls, Formica-topped tables, and rock 'n' roll music took their place as part and parcel of teens' beloved hangouts.

With the arrival of summer, many teens exchanged those walls and tables and jukeboxes for sand and blankets and radios. The beach *and* its parking lot took over as the gathering spot, and many a stretch of white sand was spotted with long rows of gaily colored beach towels anchored by antennaed radios, well-thumbed movie magazines, Coppertone bottles—and bodies ranging in color from rare to well done. By night the sands were ringside seats for crowds of submarine race watchers; beach parties complete with bonfires, more radios, blankets, a few handsome lifeguards for local color, dancing, and drinking ranked very high as a "neat" summer date!

And let us not forget all those dances—from record hops to sock hops to formal dances and proms where the white sport coat, pink carnation, and spaghetti-strapped "formal" held sway and where Purple People-Eaters and MTAs and Western Movies punctuated all those lindys and slow dances with just plain fun.

The fifties held fast the dream. Almost anything was possible. "When I grow up . . ." had a rosy hue to it, and dreaming was just nifty. Crushes were cool, and everyone had them; if that handsome hunk of a hall monitor didn't respond, there was always Troy Donahue and James Darren!

A very special decade characterized by an even more special innocence, the fifties and its teen life-style have been immortalized not only by Norman Rockwell but in many television programs such as *The Many Loves of Dobie Gillis* and *Ozzie and Harriet*—and, of course, the contemporary *Happy Days*—and in movies such as *Gidget* and *Beach Blanket Bingo*. No doubt it was the ginchiest of times.

The happy days lingered on into the early sixties. Movies,

I was crazy for Tony Curtis. My room was filled with movie magazines. I cut out the pictures and put them on the wall or mirror. It was part of dreaming about the future, and who you'd someday marry. *(1956)*
Donna F., North Carolina

Remember that little game where you matched the letters in your name with a boy's to see if the outcome was hate, friendship, love, or marriage? A silly doodling for study hall—but we all thought it was destiny! *(1964)*
Libby H., Connecticut

It's sort of embarrassing . . . but I would tell people I was under a sunlamp; actually it was beard rash! *(1955)*
Susan H., California

WON'T YOU WEAR MY RING?

especially drive-ins (where economy-minded double daters were not above stowing a couple in the trunk before driving through the gate), parties, sporting events, and dances were still Saturday-night's main event—as was parking, though this last was occasionally halted by good-natured "bush-whackers" out for some laughs. (The not-so-good-natured ones tended to be ex-steadies out for some revenge!)

"Going steady" evolved to "going with," and pairs remained a stable feature of the early sixties landscape. What *was* new was the amount of sexual activity—however surreptitious. Frenzied whispers between classes escalated dramatically.

There were quantum leaps. Soda was now altogether tame and beer was altogether a blast—as were the infrequent harder spirits. The antics were merrier than ever. Going out "drinking with the girls," a racier sister of the slumber party, conferred status upon participators (usually seniors in states where the drinking age was eighteen) and announced to the world that it was perfectly okay *not* to have a date on a weekend night. There lay adventure in running into a group of boys who were similarly inclined.

But for all the leaps, early sixties teens were still pretty traditional. Happiness was being a big frog in a little pond called the high school, hearing "Pomp and Circumstance" played for *you*, and watching the sun come up after partying all night at graduation with that one special person.

It wouldn't be that easy again for a long time. With 1964 came the whirlwind, and tradition was just one of the many things that flew right out the window as the sexual revolution and the Age of Permissiveness strode through the front door. The Pill and the rampant spirit of rebelliousness were a heady combination, blowing to smithereens all those labels and constraints of earlier years. All of a sudden it was just fine to love the one you were with simply because you felt like it. The funny part about it all was all that freedom brought with it a new pressure to conform. Many elected not to, for the price was just too high.

But the mood had changed, and it was hard not to be affected by what was going on all around you. As the sixties wore on, the usual entertainments were put down as square, uncool. The necessity to have a date on weekends ebbed. You could, like, well, hang out, get stoned, whatever; any-

If you had curlers in your hair Saturday afternoon, that meant something. It meant you had a date. *(1960)*
Arlene B., Washington

I used to baby-sit. My boyfriend would come over—but no one knew about it! *(1962)*
Carolyn H., Maine

Didn't it seem as if every girl wore Shalimar or Ambush in the sixties? But Ambush smelled a lot like my Canoe. *(1964)*
Nat H., New York

1950s

1963

1950s

The perfect excuse for a hickey: I caught my
neck in the zipper of my Jaeger sweater. (1963)
Barby H., Connecticut

1920s

1940s

1963

Saturday night's main event: a dance.

1950s

I always dated football players...
they walked different, you know,
like with a bounce. I loved it!
(1967)   Eileen V., South Dakota

thing and everything was cool. If you wanted to dance, you didn't need the gym; you simply stood up at a rock concert and did your thing—as the spirit or substance moved you; a partner or date was superfluous! There were plenty of parties, plenty of music, plenty of smoke—and plenty of grim determination to have a time like no other. It wasn't always fun but it seemed like it had to *be*.

As the constraints vanished, so did some of the distance between the sexes; the sort of friendships that might once have been unthinkable now blossomed, born of things as simple as a shared interest in, say, Led Zeppelin. You didn't have to be boyfriend and girlfriend to be tight.

These were nonetheless frenzied, confusing times. The signals came from numerous directions. But where the boys were was still where the girls were—anywhere from a movie or a rock concert to a keg party. It was a hard day's night.

When morning came, roundabout 1971, the world looked clearer and quieter. Word even had it that a return to the fifties was imminent! In spirit, anyway. All that going against the grain hadn't exactly been for naught; teens were older and wiser for the experience—and ready to take life a bit slower. It was time to have a good time of one's *own* making.

Parties were nothing but make-out sessions, usually in the basement. Lights out! *(1969)*
Tony R., Maryland

Alcohol resumed its place as the favorite libation, and wine crept in to rival beer as an easy drink. Parties with *dancing* returned, as did dressing up and going out—just like they used to do!

Slumber party!

1963

The pendulum continued its slow swing through the mid-seventies as the Me Decade appeared in serious danger of expiring due to exhaustion. The legacy of the sixties, the sexual revolution, had created a generation who had skipped all the fun stuff and gone right to the game. All the anachronisms like dating, romance, and courtship began to look mighty enticing and, well, excellent!

Now there are discos to go to and dance the night away. A happy legacy of the sixties is that you don't have to have a date; in fact, it can be a downright handicap! And there are punk and new wave clubs for which it is a real kick to dress outrageously for the night—even if morning means a return to slightly more conservative dress.

Conservative, too, is the social scene. Many teens are opting for going out in groups rather than dating exclusively. Some observers point to the economy as a partial reason for the new seriousness. A concern with their work and future is creasing a lot of young brows and tempering extracurricular activities.

The seventies played host to one very important change that seems in no danger of being ephemeral. Girls are asking boys for dates, and a joyful, husky-voiced chorus of "It's about time!" must be the best endorsement possible.

Twenties, thirties, forties, fifties, sixties, seventies, eighties. . . . Whatever the time, whatever your pleasure—those were the days!

Instead of going to the movies with a date, guys and girls go shopping together. It's fun! Bet they didn't do that in the forties. *(1983)* *Lorraine M., New York*

My parents are always saying that we move too fast—that we're already doing things, like dating, going to places, and trying things long before they did it. *(1983)*

Pat S., California

1947

'TWIXT

1960s

1980s

If a girl asks me out, I think that's great. They should have done that years ago instead of being so old-fashioned. *(1983) Donald S., Virginia*

Do Ya, Do Ya Wanna Dance?

When we danced it was like the only way we could get real close. Like talking without saying anything— I used to let Sinatra speak for me. *(1948)*
Roland J., Illinois

Gimme the Stones—in concert! *(1982)*
Sally G., Pennsylvania

From the shimmy of the twenties to the bop and twist of the sixties to the freestyle of the eighties, each generation of teenagers has created its own special style of dancing. The rest of the population is usually jolted at the outset and characteristically responds by casting an all too critical eye—until they've had a chance to try it themselves!

Jazz, which made its first significant appearance around 1910, constituted the background for most of the teenage dance crazes until rock 'n' roll pushed it out of the way in the fifties. Jazz was regarded as the true spirit of joyous revolt from convention, custom, authority—and boredom. And it most certainly celebrated the feelings of the twenties' generation of Flaming Youth. It was so popular, in fact, that many high schools and colleges had their own student jazz bands.

The Roaring Twenties ushered in totally new dance steps and music. Ragtime, hot jazz, Dixieland, and zany dances like button shining and the shimmy, where partners quivered like bowls of Jell-O, captured perfectly the mood of this "no holds barred" decade.

Prior to 1920, cheek-to-cheek dancing—and kissing in public—signaled immediate plans for marriage, so the turnaround at the hands of Flaming Youth was especially dramatic. Thousands of flappers yanked off their corsets before jumping onto the dance floor. Young men, in a previously *unthinkable* move, put their hands on the bare skin of their partners—who now wore low-backed dresses—while they wiggled away the night to "Toot Toot Tootsie Goodbye" and "Makin' Whoopie."

The biggest craze of the twenties was a dance that came straight from James P. Johnson's New York musical, *Runnin' Wild*. The kicky, fast-stepped Charleston quickly replaced button shining and left dancers too pooped to be passionate. At the same time, novelty dances like the black bottom, the sugar foot strut, and the varsity drag kept partners gasping.

The popular song titles of the decade captured all that bubbly exuberance about dating, fun, and sex: "Yes Sir! That's

We used to dance the two-step. We'd go over to someone's house, play the piano, sing, and dance the two-step. Very nice. (1924) Albert H., New York

I used to go over to this girl Martha's house, and she tried teaching me to dance. I wasn't very good—clumsy. Anyway, we did the two-step to "Stardust." (1929) Derek H., Minnesota

You could see that Charleston dance step being practiced everywhere you went—waiting for a bus, even in the school hallways. Nothing like the Charleston beat. (1928) Alice J., New York

1950s

1944

1940s

My Baby"; "Gimme a Little Kiss, Will Ya Huh?"; "Runnin'
Wild"; "Ain't We Got Fun"; "Five Foot Two, Eyes of Blue—
Has Anybody Seen My Gal?" and "Baby Face."

But one could be out of breath for just so long. The thirties
saw music ease up, slide back a bit, and definitely go mellow.
Swing and sweet music and big bands were all the rage. In
1934 Glen Gray and the Casa Loma Orchestra led the pack,
but by 1936 Benny Goodman was king. Swing tastes varied
across the country; the South preferred graceful dance
rhythms, while the East favored the tempos of Tommy and
Jimmy Dorsey, not to mention Goodman.

Even in the depths of the Depression, when attendance
at school dances and proms dropped sharply, the big bands
remained busy. While Rudy Vallee and his group charged
Yale a whopping $1650 in 1937, other schools, rather than
eliminate the name bands, instituted various economy meas-
ures. Dances were moved from downtown hotels to school
gyms, and decorations ran to crepe paper and lots of imagination. Favors were eliminated, and many boys agreed not
to buy corsages for their dates.

But dance they did—the big apple and the shag and a
host of others. A new style of jazz flowed from the radio waves
to the ballrooms; and Betty Hutton and the face-to-face jig—
or jitterbug—burst onto the scene. In a version known as the
lindy hop, jitterbug partners flashily demonstrated breaka-
ways and fancy swing-outs—and looked to all the world as
if they were dancing by themselves.

The thirties may be synonymous with hard times, but
those hard times were all the more reason to try and find
some good times—and to make *those* moments as light-
hearted as humanly possible.

Teens jitterbugged on through the early forties, while
those in uniform found a peaceful interlude in the fox-trot,
the lindy, and the waltz. But as the war wore on, bands and
ballrooms went bankrupt, and dancing all but went out of
style for a time. At the war's end, big bands did not make a
comeback; instead, combos made an auspicious entrance
and quickly took their place as the favorite bands for dances
and proms.

An even more auspicious debut was made in 1942 when
Frank Sinatra opened at the Paramount in New York City.
Swooning, squealing, and general bedlam attended every

1922

1950s

Next dance is a ladies' choice!

performance of "The Voice"—so much so that ushers carried smelling salts and manned stretchers! "Sinatritis" infected millions of bobby-soxers while confounding an equal number of adults, who simply couldn't understand the appeal of this unlikely idol. But looks aside, the Hoboken, New Jersey crooner had one great set of pipes.

In 1948, the plastic 45-rpm and long-playing 33-rpm records rendered obsolete the old 78-rpm standby, and the jukebox industry mushroomed into a 400,000-box business! At the top of the charts were Buddy Clark's "Ballerina," Perry Como's "Haunted Heart," and Frank Sinatra's "I've Got a Crush on You." Old-fashioned romance had survived the war.

Later in the decade jukeboxes went international, as it were, and added such Latin rhythms as samba, conga, mambo, and tango songs. Perez Prado's "Mambo Jambo," "Cherry Pink and Apple Blossom White," and "Patricia" were all million sellers!

And then came the fifties. Early in the decade a Cleveland disc jockey stumbled onto something that would eventually revolutionize teenage music and dance: rock and roll. When Alan Freed learned that teenagers were buying records by black rhythm-and-blues groups in staggering quantities, he decided to play a few of the records on the air. The response was more than overwhelming; it was utterly sensational. Overnight Freed coined the phrase "rock 'n' roll" to describe not only a new breed of music and dance but a whole life-style. Now Freed shouted, "Go, man, go!" and, "Yeah, yeah, yeah!" on the air. The relentless beat and the inherently sexual nature of the music did not fail to stir the teen audience, and Freed aided and abetted the rebellion against parents and established mores.

The first big rock 'n' roll hit was the legendary "Rock Around the Clock" by Bill Haley and the Comets in 1955. It was not only a smash success, it was the first song to strike teenagers as existing strictly for them. From then on, rock 'n' roll would always belong to the young.

From the South came rhythm and blues, a heady and rich tradition which helped to mold the new music's style. Artists like Chuck Berry, B. B. King, Fats Domino, Jerry Lee Lewis, Joe Turner, and Little Richard carried R & B to high art and won instant favor from electrified teen audiences.

Nothing worse than dancing. I hated it. Girls went crazy if a fellow knew how to spin them around. I thought it was silly—and still do. (1947)
Larry B., North Carolina

My "Rock Around the Clock" record was so scratched up, but we still played it. Someone cracked it at a party, but we turned it up so loud that you couldn't even hear the click, click, click. (1955)
Helene Y., Kentucky

American Bandstand was the greatest! We watched it every day. I wanted to move to Philadelphia. Anyway, I remember Fran and Mike with those big eyes, and Yvette and her sister Carmen with the blond streak. (1959)   Lisa G., Ohio

Too pooped to be passionate!

1920s

1938

939

1944

Jitterbug!

'TWIXT

1940s

My two favorites were Kenny and Justine. Weren't they everybody's? *(1958)*
Robert S., Virginia

Funny how two girls could dance together and it was okay. But two guys—never happen. *(1958)* *Vincent E., Oregon*

I hated it when the disc jockey at the hop would call for a Ladies' Choice. Sometimes I'd have to sit it out, so then I'd go for a cigarette with a bunch of other guys. *(1959)*
Elliot R., Louisiana

Millions of young people were up and dancing, to the irresistible beat of rock 'n' roll bands and records. On Dick Clark's *American Bandstand* teens danced variations of the same jitterbug that had been around for decades, but now there was all sorts of excitement. It was on camera! *Bandstand*, which originated in Philadelphia, turned every teenager's head and hips. By 1958 it was the number one daytime TV show. *American Bandstand* teens set trends; they taught teens how to lindy and bop, and invented three new dances— the stroll, the circle, and a modified cha-cha called the chalypso. In cities across the country record hops were the rage and quickly became Friday- and Saturday-night celebrations. Schools picked up on the idea, occasionally modifying it. One version was called a sock hop, because teens held dances in the gym and shed their saddle shoes to avoid scratching the floor! And there were the special numbers— The Spotlight Dance, Ladies' Choice, and Statues, where dancers had to hold their positions when the music was interrupted, since any subsequent movement eliminated a couple from the dance.

Everyone needed a break from the fast and tricky steps, of course, and it was here, in the lights-down-low, slow-dance country that one man was king. Johnny Mathis, whose "Misty," "Chances Are," "The Twelfth of Never," and "All the Time" made an awful lot of hearts turn somersaults, could be counted on to sing exactly those romantic things that teenagers were too shy to say themselves.

The fifties saw a lot of kings and even more princes, but there was only room for one king of kings—the incomparable Elvis Presley. Hips aswivel, eyes lidded heavily, the king from Memphis strode onto the American stage and claimed it for himself. There had never been anyone like him: a white man who had the black sound and the black feel. American teens swooned—and kept on swooning—as the "king" turned out record after fabulous record. "Hound Dog," "Love Me Tender," "Any Way You Want Me," and "I Want You, I Need You, I Love You," not to mention dozens of others, hit the top of the charts and stayed and stayed. Presley pumped eroticism into the dancing with his music and his movements, and the prevailing style became known as bop, a fusion of the lindy and the jitterbug.

It was not for nothing that the music charts listed the Top

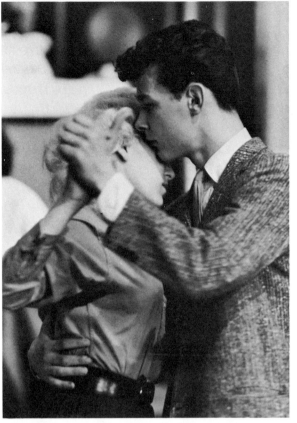

1958

1969

1978

40, rather than 10 or 20; there were hundreds of records out at any given time. A music scorecard would have been extremely useful, but most teens relied upon their local DJs to provide them with an annual trip down memory lane at Christmas and New Year's to hear the likes of all the old faves like Dion and the Belmonts, Buddy Knox, Fabian, Bobby Rydell, the Lettermen, Pat Boone, James Brown, the Platters, Little Anthony and the Imperials, Ruby and the Romantics, the Everly Brothers, Fats Domino, Brenda Lee, Jimmie Rodgers, and Connie Francis. They rocked on to the beat and tried to keep abreast of hits like "Tutti Frutti," "Blueberry Hill," "Charlie Brown," "Whole Lotta Shakin' Goin' On," "Ain't That a Shame?" "Tears on My Pillow," and "That'll Be the Day." Rock 'n' roll was a state of mind!

In 1958 the state of the art was stereo. Although a tremendous improvement over the familiar hi-fi, stereo was an expensive improvement, and teens did not immediately rush out en masse to purchase new record players and records. By 1960, however, the big boxes with the separate speakers were rapidly displacing the old hi-fi as essential furniture in a teenager's room. What? Listen to Brenda Lee's "I'm Sorry" in mono? Yucky.

The stars came and went—though more than a few departed prematurely. A plane crash in 1959 claimed the lives of Buddy Holly, Richie Valens, and the Big Bopper—the first of many accidents that would leave the music world and its devoted young audience poorer and which would remind them that there was indeed a darker side to life.

If the late fifties proved to be a music ground swell, the early sixties marked a crossroads. Groups like the Kingston Trio, the Brothers Four, and the Chad Mitchell Trio had been drawing college and high school students like magnets, with folk songs like "The Sloop John B," "Green Fields," and "Last Night I Had the Strangest Dream." Rock 'n' roll held fast, to be sure, but the crowds lured by the likes of Bob Dylan, Joan Baez, Pete Seeger, Odetta, and Buffy Sainte-Marie were impressive. The hootenanny (or gathering of folksingers) made for popular entertainment, and thousands descended upon Newport, Rhode Island, each summer for the incomparable Newport Folk Festival. Lest there be any doubt about radio play of folk songs, suffice it to say that numbers like Peter, Paul and Mary's "If I Had a Hammer" and the Kingston Trio's

"Tom Dooley" and "Scotch and Soda" remained on the charts for sometimes as long as two years!

The Midwest, specifically Motor City! (or Detroit) cultivated its own special sound, known as Motown, and harvested a stunning crop of artists: Diana Ross and the Supremes, Smokey Robinson and the Miracles, the Four Tops, the Ronettes, Marvin Gaye, the Temptations, Martha and the Vandellas, and many more.

In 1961 a dance that would eventually be seen and heard round the world was born in Philadelphia, its creator a plump teenager whose singing and dancing were the toast of his neighborhood. Chubby Checker's twist, an immediate hit, became rock 'n' roll's first long-standing dance craze. Certainly no dance has ever ignited such a furor! Critics fumed and sputtered, psychologists compared, and academics searched for links, while its creator referred breezily to TV shows like *Ramar of the Jungle* and native dances. Such a to-do over a dance in which partners did not even touch! Meanwhile, teenagers just plain loved it.

The twist swept the nation, spawning a commercial explosion (twist chairs, shoes, candy, hairdos, dresses, etc.), and before long, a wide assortment of related dances: the Fly, the Loco-Motion, the Mashed Potato, the Slop, the Pony, the Dirty Bird, the Monkey, the Swim. The list kept on growing as the Bossa Nova, the Wobble, the Bug, the Frug, the Dog, the Slurp, the Watusi, the Hully Gully, the Boogaloo, the Surfer, the Philly Jerk, the Shingaling, and the Bristol Stomp pushed the others out of the way.

As if keeping up with American steps was not enough, in 1963 Trinidad exported the Limbo and suddenly teens were asking "How low can you go?" as they bent backwards and edged carefully under a limbo pole.

In 1964 we looked to France for inspiration and borrowed the discotheque (record library), where dancers could disport themselves to very loud recorded music. The discotheque was not so much innovative as it was a chic Gallic sister to the fifties record hop. The dance floors, small and crowded at the best of times, gave rise to movements that could be performed while virtually standing still.

If you were a teenager in 1964, however, you undoubtedly had something infinitely less French and decidedly more exciting on your mind, for it was then that the Beatles' music

It was hard dancing to the Kingston Trio. I loved to listen to them, tap my fingers and feet, and sing along. I guess that's the way you danced to their music. *(1960)*
        Carl F., Pennsylvania

Guess how I learned to do the twist? I pretended I was drying myself off with a towel and just rubbed my rear end. It worked! *(1962)*   *Kevin D., Iowa*

We went to square dances. I did things like the 'scoot back' and the 'curlique.' That's when you make like a wave. *(1962)*
        Ben J., Arkansas

Discotheque dancing was the best. Nice thing about it was the floor was so crowded no one could see what you were doing! *(1965)*   *Rodney W., Kentucky*

1960s

'TWIXT

1957

hit our shores, to be followed shortly by its creators. Talk about ground swell! The turf was so right for the arrival of John, Paul, Ringo, and George. They generated more enthusiasm and activity in the music world and among the young than any group or individual—including Elvis! Teens flocked to record stores in such numbers that "I Want to Hold Your Hand" drew more than a million customers within ten days of its issue. The hits kept on coming: "Can't Buy Me Love," "Twist and Shout," "She Loves You," "Please Please Me," and many, many more. It was love at first sight and a love that would endure.

The Beatles were the leaders of a sizable pack. Following close on their heels were other British groups like Herman's Hermits, Gerry and the Pacemakers, the Dave Clark Five, the Who, and the other legend, the Rolling Stones.

By the late sixties the student movement and the escalating war in Vietnam, among other factors, had a lot to do with a music revolution of sorts. Singles had given way to albums as AM Top 40 had to FM underground sound, both of which had a powerful effect on teen dancing. Slowly but surely it receded. Flower children *listened* to music. Parties meant lots of teens arrayed against the shadowy walls of a room, digging the acid rock on the stereo, and passing joints and water pipes.

Their music heroes included a few familiar names like Joan Baez, Judy Collins, Bob Dylan, and the Beatles, and scores of new ones: Jim Morrison and the Doors, Janis Joplin, Cream, Moody Blues, Santana, Grateful Dead, Mothers of Invention, David Bowie, Elton John, Crosby, Stills and Nash, Neil Young, Simon and Garfunkel, Jimi Hendrix, Led Zeppelin, and Jefferson Airplane.

The music reflected a lot more than a preoccupation with "moon and June" romance; it was riddled with concern over social problems like war, racism, poverty, and a not-so-healthy concern with psychotropic drugs: "Blowin' in the Wind," "A Horse With No Name," "Light My Fire," "Soul Sacrifice," "Bridge Over Troubled Waters," "A Question of Balance," "With a Little Help from My Friends," "Lucy in the Sky with Diamonds," "Space Oddity," "Southern Man," "Take It to the Limit," "Casey Jones," "Dance to the Music," "Rocket Man."

Concerts became a way of life, particularly those at the

Kids walked around shaking their heads and singing 'Oooooh' like Paul McCartney. *(1964)*
Herb G., Pennsylvania

I was into the Monkees, the Dave Clark Five, and Silver Satin Wine! *(1966)*
Susan V., Michigan

Can't you remember seeing girls who acted like go-go girls? Like they were trying to freak you out on the dance floor. *(1968)*
Ralph D., Colorado

There was a battle of the bands almost every weekend. We'd dance with strobe lights going, Day-Glo posters all around, and slides projected on the wall—all that stuff. *(1969)*
Barry B., Massachusetts

Fillmore auditoriums, East *and* West. The most astounding and unexpected musical event of the decade was the Woodstock Rock Festival, to which 300,000 young people swarmed lemminglike in 1969. They came together peacefully in open fields, without benefit of adequate food, shelter, or facilities, but it seemed not to matter. What did count was that the young—hippies, straights, musicians, students, pot smokers, acidheads, whatever—were there and together, singing and dancing and listening to *their* music gurus. It was Woodstock Nation.

When they danced, they kept at arm's length; the style was less trendy than it was individual—a compilation of lots that had gone before. There hadn't been a dance craze in years.

By the mid-seventies the ground was too fertile; it had to happen and it did. Dancing was back! You had to stay at arm's length—ten feet, even—but dancing was hot, in, and everyone was doing it. Discos, a much snappier and bigger version of the sixties discotheques, lit up cities across America to the dawn's early light. It was essential that you spent a lot of time getting ready for a night at a disco; consequently, the action didn't really pick up until eleven or twelve. Partners weren't even necessary; no one could tell who was with whom in the crush. What was important was to stand out, glitter, shine—and dance to the records of the high priestess of the scene, Donna Summer. The dances were long, the gyrations indescribably complex when suddenly, *pairs* began to look good again. Two was a show!

When the Australian group, the Bee Gees, made their enormous comeback in the mid-seventies with "Stayin' Alive," the main song title from the all-time disco movie, *Saturday Night Fever*, not only was pair dancing again enshrined but *formation* dances were back. Hello fifties—with a difference!

Teens high-stepped through the hustle, whose beat was none other than the mambo, and they touched more and more. The rebellious spirit raised its head again around 1977 when England exported punk and its antiheroes, Sid Vicious and Johnny Rotten. Now the graceful moves were out and harsh was in. For the pogo, dancers jumped up and down as if riding a pogo stick; for slam dancing, they went for aggressive body contact and slammed into one another. Ouch!

Concerts were always a gas. The music was so loud it just wiped everything else out! *(1970)*
George H., California

1964

1960s

But harsh is rarely palatable over time, so it was inevitable that something a little easier and less razor-edged would supplant punk. New wave, with its retro look (the fifties again!) and an overlay of punk fit the bill perfectly. Groups like the Boomtown Rats and Blondie soared in popularity and were joined by eighties originals like the Go-Gos. Yet underneath all the *new* music lies a rock 'n' roll soul that is unmistakable. "The more things change," the prophet said...

As if to reflect that strong rock 'n' roll heritage, the dance style of the eighties is a rich combination of jitterbug, disco, and the current freestyle.

Today's teens rock on, as do yesterday's teens—their parents!

Of course we dance today, but we don't have all those names for it. Just smile and move. *(1983)*
Gloria F., Michigan

I go to a place where they play all kinds of *great* old-fashioned stuff like tangos and sambas and mambos. It's terrific! *(1983)*
Lynn B., New York

DO YA, DO YA WANNA DANCE?

"You just stood up and did your own thing."

1970s

'TWIXT

1960s

1960s

DO YA, DO YA WANNA DANCE?

Everyone's Doing It

I was wild about mood rings, big box radios, and painters' pants. The girls wore shag cuts, or the layered look, and we all loved Elton John. *(1973)*

Margaret H., California

If you sat down and made a list of all the crazy, zany, and fun fads of this century, well, you could write a book!

A fad is rather like a stamp of approval—at least among teenagers, who often value sameness. Call it conformity if you like. Whatever it is, a fad is meant to be fun—a blast to join, but better yet, a real kick to be the first to try!

The mood of the country in the 1920s was particularly conducive to fads. Scores of them swept the nation as the newly minted teenagers moved into high gear. After all, those in-between years were there to enjoy! Crossword puzzles, yo-yos, mah-jongg, roller skating, Hi-Li, and marathons of all kinds—the enthusiasm was boundless. Teens everywhere competed among themselves to set a trend or two.

Endurance contests led the pack. In 1929 Baltimore became the unofficial center of flagpole sitters. Inspired by one Alvin "Shipwreck" Kelly, the original flagpole master, fifteen-year-old Avon Foreman touched off the mad craze when he perched himself atop an eighteen-foot tree in his backyard. In a single week, Baltimore witnessed twenty pole sitters trying to break each other's records. The mania spread rapidly. Camden, New Jersey, police had their hands full when they counted sixty boys perched in a single tree!

The fads kept on coming. Teens had lots of time for rocking-chair derbies, cross-country races, pea-eating contests, kissing and talking marathons, bridge, gum-chewing and peanut-pushing contests. One young man with a mission attempted to push a peanut with his nose across the state of Kentucky!

Many teen stalwarts danced their way to near exhaustion in Roaring Twenties dance marathons. Substantial cash prizes—as much as a thousand dollars—spurred them on. Some simply wanted to impress their friends. On June 10, 1928, ninety-one couples entered an around-the-clock dance contest in New York's Madison Square Garden. Twenty days later, when the city's Board of Health stepped in to end it, only nine waltzing couples remained—in varying states of

This is going to sound silly. In the twenties you were a big shot if you owned a Columbia bicycle. *(1923)*
Joseph W., New York

1929

1958

1961

Top left, Avon Foreman atop his flagpole; *right*,
the fad that ran rings around...; *bottom*, boy-
to-girl talkathon: only 188 hours to go!

exhaustion. Collapse was probably more like it! There were marathon dance contests that ran to a hundred days or more, and there were dark sides to these grueling affairs: an occasional contestant expired. For twenties' teens, however, the dance marathon was delightfully emblematic of their newfound life-style—unchaperoned dating, jazz, and the Charleston.

Even though times were tough in the next decade, that ineffable teen spirit buoyed the thirties. Somehow teens found plenty to do to release tensions and divert anxieties. Although endurance contests remained popular, bicycling, roller skating, Monopoly, Ping-Pong, bridge, card games like Hearts and Michigan, and charades were the favorites. During the 1920s millions of homes buzzed with the sound of radio for the very first time. By 1939, *The Lone Ranger*, which began in 1933, was heard by twenty-two million people three times a week! Teens also tuned in to hear President Roosevelt's "Fireside Chats" and Joe Louis' boxing matches.

Another humorous sign of the times was the teenage fascination with popular jokes:

> "Knock, knock."
> "Who's there?"
> "Wanda."
> "Wanda who?"
> "Wanda buy a nice apple?"

By 1939, teens were ripe for another round of wild and nutty fads. The chilling art of goldfish swallowing attracted the public's eye on March 3 at Harvard University, in Cambridge, Massachusetts. Freshman Lothrop Withington, Jr., demonstrated his fishy act on a $10 bet. The news hit the nation's campuses like a tidal wave, and students immediately tried to eat one better! At the University of Pennsylvania in Philadelphia, one enterprising undergraduate gulped 25, while a sophomore at St. Mary's University set a record by downing 210 squiggly fishies!

The fads craze took a somewhat different turn with platters of a phonographic variety. And when Frank "Swoonatra" broke out in 1943 with songs like "Snooty Little Cutie" and "How Do You Do Without Her?" there just didn't exist a supply of 78s large enough for his teen audience. And those records, in turn, became an essential ingredient of yet another fad—

My partner and I tried chewing celery to stay awake (you couldn't chew gum). We'd take breaks every so often and rest on the cots alongside the dance floor. *(1929)*

Hugh B., Massachusetts

If your feet weren't moving, you were disqualified from the dance contest. So we all did some 'lugging.' That's when you hang on to your partner and sway a little. *(1930)*

Mollie F., Maryland

slumber parties. Giggling and gabbing the night away was that much better if one's favorite crooner was spinning on the Victrola!

The war interrupted all that carefree chatter, and young people were soon preoccupied with matters more important. Some waited for the draft, others volunteered, and girls kept themselves busy writing letters and mailing packages to GIs. Of necessity, fads faded a bit.

They returned with a vengeance in the fifties. The battle of the sexes was on! Campuses across the country rang with war cries like "Drop your panties!" and "We want sex!" In fact, some very cooperative girls were more than willing to toss not only their panties but their bras and slips out the window to the eager crowd below. Earlier decades had witnessed such spectacles, but none were so fervent as those in the fifties.

But the fad that ran rings, you should pardon the expression, around them all was the Hula-Hoop. While it may sound as if it bears a Hawaiian heritage, the Hula-Hoop was actually born in Australia, where high-school students used them to keep in shape. In 1958 the Hula-Hoop made its way across the Pacific, and overnight became the national pasttime. The colored plastic hoops were everywhere—at parties, on beaches, even in school. Sales hit more than $45 million in 1959, and approximately thirty million hoops were sold before the fad took a tumble into obscurity—however temporary. It surfaced ten years later for another brief round.

You could say that the fifties also marked a new way of looking at things. Teens ducked behind sunglasses to eye each other and the rest of the world. Squares, polygons, and oblongs transformed a lot of young faces, but the more daring purchased flair in a variety of exotic shapes, dazzling colors, and adornments ranging from gilt stars to plastic flowers— or flamingos!

On November 26, 1952, a movie called *Bwana Devil* opened in Los Angeles and broke box-office records in its first week by grossing $95,000. What was truly remarkable about this otherwise unremarkable film was that the audience had to wear special glasses to watch it. For *Bwana Devil* was a 3-D (the name given to a type of optical illusion that turns two-dimensional images into three-dimensional ones) movie or a "deepie." Teens were positively enthralled.

Listen, here's what we did at slumber parties. We stole pants and bras from a sleeping girl's suitcase, dunked them in water, and put them in the refrigerator. The trick was to replace them secretly the next morning—then let her try to put them on! *(1945)*
Tracy D., Tennessee

I took part in a panty raid once. We collected an awful lot of black, white, and beige lacy little numbers. The next day we spread them out on the lawn near the dorms so the girls could claim them. Lots of guys kept some; I know I did! *(1953)*
Bernie P., Massachusetts

We took it one further. We Hula-Hooped on the Bongo Board! Talk about coordination striking back. *(1958)*
Chris C., Wisconsin

The Hula-Hoop was a *waist* of time! *(1959)*
Craig S., New York

1979

'TWIXT

1922

1980s

1980s

Sounds of the times.

Hondo and a spate of others followed, but the fad was short-lived. Those glasses were a nuisance! The eighties, oddly enough, have seen 3-D reemerge, and this time it appears destined to stay. Not only have fifties' movies—and glasses—captured the fancy of today's audiences, but the new technology is such that the 3-D effect can be had without the glasses and is sure to play an important part in movies and television.

The year 1958 witnessed the birth of something very close to the teenager's heart and ears: the transistor radio. The space program took the bows for this great step toward twenty-four-hour rock 'n' roll. The little boxes cropped up everywhere, but nowhere was the battle of the bands—fifties style—more intense than on the nation's beaches.

The popularity of rock 'n' roll stars produced all sorts of fads and fancies. Elvis was king, and products bearing his name, image, or signature flooded stores everywhere. Teen collectors were busy sorting through hats, T-shirts, kerchiefs, bobby sox, sneakers, purses, billfolds, charm bracelets, autograph books, lipsticks, hound dog pillows, stationery, greeting cards, glow-in-the-dark pictures of Elvis, and, of course, records.

Endurance tests and marathons reappeared in the fifties and sixties. The increased use of the telephone soon qualified it as an extension of a teenager's arm, so it was hardly surprising that a talkathon should follow. Just how long *could* you stay on the phone? In 1961 a group at Western Michigan University in Kalamazoo took turns keeping one phone going for 124 hours in a six-day relay; their success spurred on more teens, many of whom kept it rather informal by restricting themselves to the family phone!

It required a lot more than one teen, however, to indulge in some of the decade's other fads. Teens stuffed themselves into any worthy receptacle they could find. Fifty-five students at Colorado State University in Fort Collins made headlines when they crammed themselves into an old hearse; others chose the Volkswagen bug as the favorite target.

There was more. Some students stuffed their rooms with newspaper, while in 1964 teens at the University of Oklahoma in Norman stacked a record fifty-six people on a single bed! But surely the most celebrated stuffing fad was the telephone booth. Each week saw last week's record broken. Thirty-five

1959

26

1950s

EVERYONE'S DOING IT

79

1952

young people squeezed into a booth at Southern State in Magnolia, Arkansas, in 1959, yet others claimed to have pushed the numbers higher. The bigger question remained unanswered: Who paid for the call?

While so many were busy stuffing, a couple of teenagers in Indiana had a cool idea of their own—dancing with an ice cube on the bridge of their noses! Jeanie Englebright and Kent Wilson gave it a whirl and clocked fifteen and three-quarter minutes.

While Jeanie and Kent probably danced to Johnny Mathis, West Coast teens were tuning in to the Beach Boys in 1961. The California surf had teenagers by the thousands shooting curls and hanging ten, piling into woodies, and following the "big ones." But there came to pass days when the surf was just not up, so what was a hotdogger to do? Why, bolt a few skate wheels to tapered pieces of wood, of course. Voila, the skateboard! Enthusiasts were dubbed "asphalt athletes," their sport, "sidewalk surfing."

Simpler still was another fad that took its rightful place in the sun, preferably on a beach: the Frisbee. Someone even went so far as to claim that the Frisbee symbolized America's young. Millions of teens threw the plastic flying saucer wherever they found an open space, be it backyard, schoolyard, park, or beach. Certainly no car trunk was complete without one.

In the late sixties and early seventies, no teenager's room was complete without posters. If ever there was a period checkered with messages, this was it. Fillmore Auditorium posters announcing such groups as the Grateful Dead hung side by side with Peter Fonda, MAKE LOVE, NOT WAR, FLOWER POWER, and TODAY IS THE FIRST DAY OF THE REST OF YOUR LIFE. The walls fairly glowed with that riot of Day-Glo—and actually did when you turned on that ever-so-important black light. What better way to view the phantasmagoria!

The messages moved off the walls and onto buttons, stickers, and T-shirts. Lapel buttons gave teens a particularly simple and direct way of announcing their views and humor: STUDENT POWER! FREE LOVE! BLACK IS BEAUTIFUL! GIRLS SAY YES TO BOYS WHO SAY NO! WOMAN'S PLACE IS IN THE HOUSE AND THE SENATE! GIVE A DAMN!

Like the charm in the Cracker Jacks box, psychedelic posters of rock stars were frequently a freebie enclosure in record albums. Not surprisingly, these posters came to be as valuable and popular as the record itself. Before long, stores were offering posters of rock superstars, then sports superstars, and finally sex symbols like Farrah Fawcett and Cheryl Tiegs.

As the political climate cooled across the country, the need for protest messages abated, but the attraction of wearing a message—any message—held fast. T-shirts and stickers displayed photos of rock stars, hearts, rainbows, pigs, happy faces, myriad products, and such self-advertisements as YOUR PACE OR MINE? and KISS ME, I DON'T SMOKE.

While some fads made the rounds, others were coming

What made me laugh were the guys who drove around with surfboards on their cars. Now *where* did they think they were going to find the big waves in Scranton? *(1962)*
    Linda W., Pennsylvania

Do you remember Clackers? A very noisy fad in 1975.
    Wendy B., New Jersey

I had a Pet Rock. Did you? *(1975)*
    Scott H., Florida

Hey, who remembers mooning?
(1972)   Robert C., New York

You mean pressed ham? *(1965)*
Hank B., Illinois

My digital watch is programmed
for wake-up, lunch, and *General
Hospital. (1982)*
Patti T., Arizona

I can't do my homework unless
I'm wired for sound. Since it's for
my ears only, there's no grief.
(1983)   Heather W., New Jersey

I want a digital minicomputer/
TV/radio wristwatch. Everything
on a strap. *(1982)*
Esther M., New York

About the closest thing to a fad
is 'quarters,' a beer game. Flip a
coin. If it goes in the glass, you
point to someone. They have to
drink. If you miss, you drink. I
like to miss! *(1982)*
Rosemary P., New York

off. In 1974 streaking took off; the first to shed were America's college students. Embarrassment was no deterrent, and nothing, but nothing, was too sacred. The Lyndon Johnson Library, police stations, the Michigan legislature, the nationally televised Academy Awards, ski races, football games, and parties were all considered eminently fair and bare game.

A winning streak was made to be broken. Texas Tech students streaked for a record-breaking five hours, while more than fifteen hundred University of Georgia students participated in a mass streak which, when the dust and blushes had cleared, turned out to be the largest in history!

The eighties have seen the arrival of E.T.: electronic teenager. Now teens trade in the real world for one that plays to them through their portable headset stereos—between classes, on the way home, in the car, while doing homework. Digital watches have also joined the parade of teen fadtronics. Nothing less than a control panel for every young wrist!

Teens' hand and eye coordination has been fine tuned by a bevy of microcoaches with the unlikely names of Pac-Man, Donkey Kong, Defender, Centipede, and Tron. The video arcade has become the Pleasure Island of the eighties. Pinocchio and his boys would have loved it!

But video games are not limited to the arcades; they've invaded the home and the television screens. When teens tire of playing Space Wars, 3-D Tic Tac Toe, and Soccer, they can always turn the channel to MTV for a little sound with their sight. Wall-to-wall mini rock concerts featuring the avant-garde Devo, the Police, the Clash, Pat Benatar, Kim Carnes, Eddie Mony, Hall and Oates, and such old and familiar names as the Stones, Fleetwood Mac, and Paul McCartney are driving teens to the max, fer shurr!

Short-lived teenage crazes have made heroes of the most unlikely celebrities of yesteryear. Recently, more than ten thousand college and high-school students joined the Official Three Stooges Fan Club to promote campus film festivals and get the Stooges' names inscribed in Hollywood's Walk of Fame. In 1982 college students on several campuses created a Beaver Cleaver cult and idolized the youngster played by Jerry Mathers in the fifties situation comedy. To pay homage, Beaver's admirers got together to drink root beer, eat Hostess Twinkies, and watch reruns of *Leave It to Beaver.* Parents were very concerned!

1963

1980s

1960s

1961

Wild and nutty fads: *above*, bed racing; *opposite*, *top*, a game of push ball at Columbia University; *bottom*, fishy acts at Harvard.

'TWIXT

1910

1939

1965

1974

1982

Winning streaks are made to be broken.

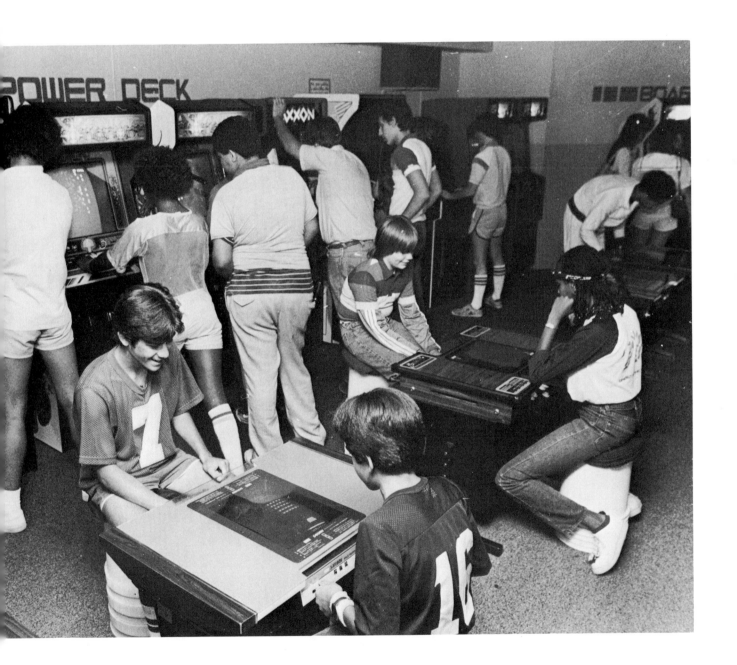

Rags to Britches

I want to thank whoever created the Banlon sweater. Very, very nice. *(1953)*
                                            Al T., Ohio

Princess Di has done a lot for ruffles. *(1983)*
                                Caroline C., Pennsylvania

Sweaters tight or bulky, Bermuda shorts, motorcycle jackets, miniskirts, designer jeans, T-shirts—teens and fashion go back a long way. Followers and leaders both, teens have always set great store by how they look—while stores have set their sights (and budgets) on catering to those looks!

The word *fashion* usually summons to mind women's clothes, so it is appropriate that we look back to the year 1919 and get off on the right (feminine) foot—with a flash of leg, of course.

The end of World War I saw the suffragette movement gain momentum and women get the right to vote. Rejoicing and rebellion followed hard on the heels of both, and feminine fashion reflected it all. In 1919 skirts went six inches above the ground; by 1920 another three more had fallen away. The twenties roared in with veritable carloads of changes, and suddenly it was youth, adolescent youth, who set the pace.

The flapper pouted her prettily painted lips (good heavens!) at the hourglass figure, the heavy fabrics, the petticoats, and, worst of all, the *corsets* of old and cried, "No more!" Bring on the rail-thin silhouettes and mere wisps of dresses that bared not only shinbones but knees!

Flappers delighted in short-sleeved or sleeveless sacklike dresses and skimpy skirts, both of which dictated that fat was out and flat, in. With glee they discarded bras (less is more, even if you have to bind it) and donned silk stockings, all the better to show off those newly exposed and sexy legs! When it came time to dress up, they opted for low-cut, tight-fitting gowns that bared lots of skin, high heels, and small cloches. Summer saw them jump into maillots or one-piece close-fitting bathing suits, and subsequently saw a lot of male pulses jump when the scantily clad girls hit the sand!

And those faces, whose shine had previously been left to Mother Nature's whims, now glittered and shone with all sorts of help from an array of cosmetics.

The clothes may have been little girl, but the look was

No, I didn't wear lipstick or makeup in school. Of course not! We were not that far along yet, and it was not allowed. *(1928)*
Frieda H., Connecticut

pure vamp. The short, waistless, or dropped waist dresses in myriad pale, thin fabrics and the large floppy bows had been copied exactly, but the heavy beads and the enormous artificial flower adornments were new and slightly naughty. The wearers sought fun and excitement at every turn.

Not for young men the settled look of an older generation either. *Their* ideal was slim and modern to match their adventuresome dispositions and romantic bents. They passed over bulky, authoritative-looking suits for shorter jackets with sloping, less padded shoulders, and high-waisted pants in lighter fabrics and colors. For informal occasions, only knickers and pullovers would do, topped off with the flat caps they'd worn as boys.

Joe College accessorized his knickers and pullover with saddle shoes and bow tie, then added a Norfolk jacket under that all-important coonskin coat. He, of course, was able to show himself off to great advantage as he drove proudly around town in his Stutz Bearcat, his ukulele or banjo on the seat beside him and his hip flask of "giggle water" tucked safely into an accommodating pocket!

Irreverent, naughty, mildly pagan, Lost Generation teens were considered very lost by some, while others, like FDR, told them in 1926: "You are more in love with life; you play with fire openly, where we did it in secret."

The skirt length hit the kneecap in 1927, but the stock market prices tumbled in 1929 and with them went hemlines, youthful frivolity, and the Lawless Decade. Depression times were not adventurous times.

For Depression-era teens, who were far more purposeful and serious than their twenties' counterparts, skirts dropped back to nearly ankle-length as fabrics veered toward the heavy and somber. If you could afford to be fashionable at all, you installed shoulder pads in coats, suits, sweaters, and blouses for the squared-shoulder, "football player" look. Everyone wore longer, heavier coats.

The same went for men. Heavier, darker, more rugged fabrics were the order of the day, and their double-breasted, full-cut jackets had square, padded shoulders, giving a more substantial appearance. Men's pants, however, hadn't been so wide in years.

But as the Depression wore on, some of the gloom wore off. Teens of both sexes elected not to differ in their casual

Like most of the girls, I always dressed up very nice for school. Usually a white blouse with a simple chain necklace. *(1925)*
Betty S., Pennsylvania

Boys looked like boys. I never wore a pink anything! *(1929)*
Harry R., Colorado

I bought a new bathing suit which showed a lot more of me. Finally, I felt like I was seventeen! *(1928)*
Sybil M., Florida

Heck, it wasn't all that depressing during the Depression. Why I can remember sewing my own clothes at home—they kept me going for a long while. *(1932)*
Barbara G., Idaho

pre 1920

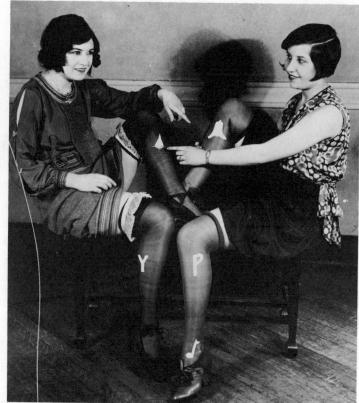

1926

1928

'TWIXT

wear. They liked their dungarees served up with sloppy shirt-tails, loose-fitting sweaters, and saddle shoes. If you were going to depart from this, best you do it in a beer jacket and shorts!

And then came the war. It was inevitable that with gas rationing and meat rationing would come a fabric rationing of sorts: cuffs, extra pockets, deep hems, and full garments were suddenly a thing of the past. The Spartan look was born.

Although the clothing reflected the mood, it did not become drab uniform; there was still enough fabric for gathered "ballerina-length" skirts bound at the waist by wide velvet belts and topped with pretty cotton blouses.

However lean, those years did give birth to an American phenomenon: bobby sox. Wartime rationing had forced stocking manufacturers to substitute rayon for nylon, but rayon proved to be a very poor second. It stretched at every wearing, necessitating frequent new purchases. Bobby sox were infinitely easier and more economical; besides, they went with almost everything!

"Almost everything," after the war, certainly included the ubiquitous jewel-necked sweater and tweed skirt ensemble so popular with teenage girls. The socks were somewhat less apparent on teenage boys, overshadowed as they were by broad-shouldered (no less than several inches of padding), wide-lapel zoot suit jackets which drooped to somewhere below the knee, and pants whose legs were the diameter of a telephone pole!

These years also witnessed teen boys imitating their GI heroes by wearing combat boots occasionally, and teen girls imitating their sophisticated older sisters by wearing lipstick and rouge more than occasionally!

After the war, teenage girls sought not to imitate but to pursue fashion that emphatically separated them from the boys: unpadded shoulders, padded bras, tight-waisted, long full skirts over crinolines, cinch belts, and high heels, depending on the occasion. (The trusty saddle shoe remained a wardrobe staple.)

And then it was 1950, the first year of the decade that would forever be linked with teenagers as *their* decade.

Fifties teens were characterized by an insatiable appetite for novelty and a desire to imitate their peers—both of which

Some girls wore lipstick on a date but wiped it off with alcohol before going home. *(1939)*
Jenny W., Virginia

Now don't you remember dressing up for the first day of school? Even if it was eighty degrees...everyone had on a fall outfit! *(1937)*
Dot E., New York

My saddle shoes had to be dirty, or I wouldn't wear them! *(1940)*
Lorraine D., Maryland

Letter sweaters and jackets—a real prize if you had one. Guys let their girls wear them if they were going out. *(1945)*
David B., Wyoming

It was a big deal to have someone in the military and wear something like a field jacket that was given to you. *(1946)*
Ben K., Oklahoma

Evening in Paris cologne! Everybody wore it. *(1949)*
Mary S., Massachusetts

I remember when we wore everything backwards, sweaters, belts—it was the style. *(1949)*
Diane K., Texas

Come on, they were always called dungarees, and hoods wore them. We all had corduroy pants or khakis. *(1953)*
James B., Pennsylvania

I lived in the Chicano section. I wore pegged pants, a black leather jacket, and French toe shoes. *(1953)*
Billy S., California

Never wore a hat. I just kept it in my pocket because it messed up my hair. *(1959)*   John K., Ohio

We were forever borrowing each other's clothes, especially for dates. My mother objected. *(1956)*
Marion F., Wisconsin

Listen, those *huuuge* petticoats were impossible. Like sitting in a school bus, I had to look out a side window to see where I was going! *(1958)*
Misty T., Connecticut

Wait...I remember trying to pick the angora hairs off my blue blazer—or else everyone knew what you had been doing! *(1950)*
Howie B., Massachusetts

caused advertisers and manufacturers to shiver with excitement. Department stores created special boutiques, and magazines appealed to a younger age group. Changes of wardrobe were seasonal and no self-respecting teen would wear the same clothes two years in a row. ("Mo-*ther*, you just don't understand!")

Christian Dior had introduced the New Look with its long, full skirt in 1947, and it did not fail to captivate teenage girls. After all, the fifties were the era of the prom, and frothy tulle gowns with tight, strapless bodices were the quintessential prom dresses. Petticoat fever abounded; those full skirts needed lots and lots of support!

Full skirts were hardly restricted to formal wear; they cropped up on campuses and in high schools across the country, more than likely as background for an appliquéd pink felt poodle or other nursery motif, which earned them their name: poodle skirt! When the circular skirt crowd changed into something more comfortable, chances are it was a pair of Bermuda shorts—plain or plaid—a blouse, a side-tied scarf, white bobby sox, sneakers, and, if the weather warranted, a blazer. When only a skirt would do, and you didn't want to hide your knees, a short kilt balanced by knee socks and loafers was the perfect solution.

There were groups and there were groups, to be sure, and at least one kept its collective eye on Hollywood and all the shapely starlets who were doing so much for tight sweaters and skirts. The pencil-thin skirt topped by a Banlon sweater with exactly three buttons left undone kept a lot of male classmates happy (counting pearls on the soft expanse of throat, no doubt). The less brave could take the safer—and bulkier—route of buttoning a Shetland cardigan up the back, while those who only stood and watched enviously while others got all the whistles could take refuge in an Oxford-cloth shirt beneath the sweater!

When the sweater set went dressy, they turned to fuzzy sweaters or soft ones decorated with all sorts of glittery bits like rhinestones and sequins and beads, and the absolutely "must have" accessory: plastic pop-it beads in pearly shades.

Messing around was best done in jeans and a man's shirt (the bigger the better). Rolling up the sleeves of one and the legs of the other was a given! By now, loafers had displaced sneakers to some extent and looked pretty nifty with

Put on your zoot and tie!

1940s

1930s

bobby sox—all in all a fitting, finishing touch to the above-mentioned "grubs."

Later in the decade the rage for cutting off those jeans and fraying the edges sent a lot of teens in search of scissors. Those in search of a neater look pulled on Jamaica shorts—which went Bermudas one higher!

The styles of the fifties came and went in rapid succession as hemlines went in one direction: up! The sack or chemise dress, which closely resembled a bag draped limply over a body, lasted barely a year. Short-lived, too, was the bubble or balloon skirt, which did not survive sitting down all that well, though for a time you dared not show your face at the prom without one. Pedal pushers, Capris, and clam diggers had bare shins in common and enjoyed a fairly long run, as did bulky sweaters, pleated skirts, car coats, madras shirt-waists, rope belts, circle pins, skorts (an early version of culottes), snuggle shirts, boat-necked sweaters, cummerbunds, colored tights, clutch purses, and sheaths.

Loafers, especially those that accommodated shiny pennies, sneakers, and flats were the favored footwear, although happiness on reaching age fourteen usually meant getting a pair of "heels" with a staggering elevation of three-quarters of an inch to wear to dances—and so to dwarf one's partner!

The partners wore their first suits—gray flannel—to dances and spiffed up the ensemble by adding a white or pink or blue button-down shirt and a classic, albeit narrow, tie with a subtle stripe or motif. All the better, of course, to separate themselves from that fifties icon, the greaser!

A look popularized by Marlon Brando in On the Waterfront, greaser garb consisted of a heavy leather jacket, a T-shirt, one sleeve of which was rolled to hold a pack of cigarettes, tapered pants, a wide black belt, black tie shoes, and maybe a motorcycle if you were lucky.

Their Joe College counterparts wore chinos with belts—or buckles across the back, button-down shirts, Ivy League caps, loafers, white bucks, brown bucks, cordovans, wing tips, and letter sweaters. The only leather they'd go near was that on a team jacket.

And let us not overlook the contribution made with blue suede shoes and the go-with-them blue pegged pants with the light blue side stitching!

The fifties contribution to unisex fashion was Bermuda

shorts. While they served as casual dress for boys and occasionally school dress for girls, quite a few brave young men attended country club dances attired in shorts, dinner jackets, knee socks, and loafers: hence Bermuda tux.

It didn't all change in 1960, but a lot of the looks that came out of the fifties were polished and tailored and moved right to the head of the class!

By 1962 teenage girls liked their silhouettes lean, their look tailored, and their hemlines solidly at midknee. They borrowed a lot from the boys in the way of shirts and sweaters and weskits in Donegal tweeds and plaids and checks, yet they found it hard to resist topping a tartan, box-pleated skirt with a big, cuddly sweater of loopy mohair! Loafers were fine with knee socks and kilts, but strap-happy flats and stockings were much more fun—and feminine.

When they played, girls looked to best-dressed boys of other decades and adopted Norfolk jackets and knickers and little-boy caps. Bermuda shorts were a fact of life, as were lean pants, often called hipsters, with hemlines that topped anklebones. Colored sneakers were much-loved footwear, but one *never* married them to a pair of socks!

When they swam, they went for broke—not to mention bare—and sported two-piece bathing suits (with little-boy shorts) that soon were pared to bikinis, a style that has stayed popular, though in recent years has gotten some competition from the high-cut maillots.

The glitter and gold were reserved for big events like dances, when even Mother's earrings could be appropriated, but teens did not lack for precious metals! Pins, signet rings, class rings, bangle bracelets, ID bracelets, and charm bracelets added dash to all those plaids and tweeds, though many a boy's sweater suffered "pulls" at the grasp of innocent little gold and silver charms.

The fare for boys was much plainer. Pullover sweaters, long-sleeved shirts, chinos, and loafers, desert boots, and sneakers filled *their* closets; the spots of bright color belonged to the occasional madras jacket, shorts, and ski parka—and the shine to narrow gold and silver belts that *had* to be buckled at the side!

And so it was with a veritable explosion that 1964 arrived to alter once and for all what had been basically unalterable. From England came the Beatles with their mop hair and

Heavens, those skirts we wore were so tight...you needed a slit in the back so you could walk. *(1960)*
Georgia J., Massachusetts

It was fashionable to wear a school ring, but you wore it facing you, then turned it around after graduation. *(1959)*
Margie J., Texas

Don't forget the Orlon sweater you wore buttoned up the back. And scatter pins! *(1962)*
Grace G., Kansas

Oh, yes, I wore those cute pillbox hats, even the white gloves. It was the Jackie Kennedy look. *(1963)* *Lynn B., Indiana*

Marginal-looking guys who wore a club or fraternity jacket ended up with nice girls. *(1961)*
Don G., Texas

1955

The minute I got out of my mother's sight, I'd roll the waistband and have a hemline where *I* wanted it! (1965)
Elaine R., New York

Tinted wire-rimmed glasses became fashionable and for the first time I didn't feel so freaky wearing glasses. (1969)
Angela N., Oregon

collarless jackets, and Mary Quant with her Mod look, and from not-so-far-off France came André Courrèges with his set-the-world-on-fire miniskirt. While an awful lot of not-so-young ladies made room in their closets for them, clearly the mini was destined for the young, what with their miles of leg and their newfound spirit of rebellion and protest.

This would be the decade of rapid social change. How easy and effective to *wear* the point you were trying to make! The miniskirt drew barrage after barrage of shots: high-school principals banned them, employers barred them, students debated them, boys and men loved them—and millions of females wore them!

England was exceptionally busy exporting to America in those days, and one of her best homegrowns was Twiggy, the waif model who captivated the fashion world and perhaps did the mostest for the mini. American teens rushed to copy her in such astounding numbers that Main Streets, USA, were awash with long-stemmed, white-stockinged, Mary Janed, short-haired, big-eyed, and mini'd girls, their little purses chock full of Yardley cosmetics for that Carnaby Street look.

The changes kept pace with the arrival of singers and

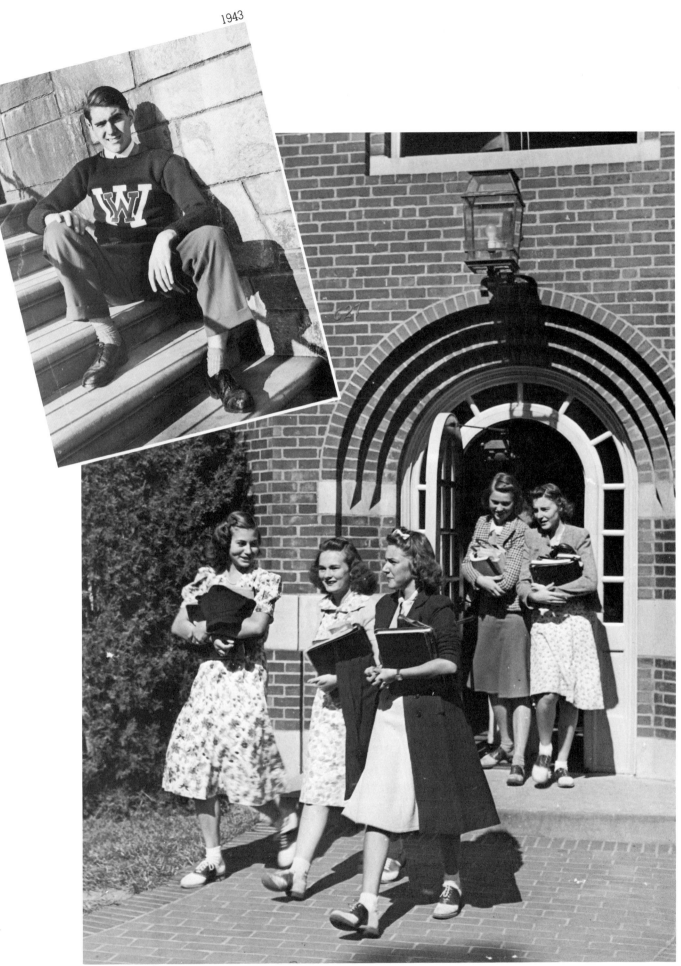

1943

1940s

bands from England. Pants, which had remained incorrigibly straight for decades, now bloomed into bell-bottoms, which looked even better when you belted them with the widest strip of leather you could find and finished it off with a shirt that told stories or bloomed like an English garden. No tailoring allowed!

The mini spawned the craze for boots which, until now, were things your mother made you wear in bad weather. Suddenly they threatened to replace shoes! Bell-bottoms all but cried for them, and certainly no member of a rock group would be caught dead without a pair—which meant that they quickly became an integral part of teens' wardrobes. The same went for blue jeans, but the older were considered the better. *They* went everywhere.

The Maginot Line had been breached during all of this: Teens shopped for the same clothes in the same stores. Unisex was alive and kicking!

The Beatles' "Sgt. Pepper's Lonely Hearts Club Band" ushered in a lot more than just a record; it opened the door on costume and fantasy dressing. Attics, thrift shops, and secondhand clothing stores were plowed through. Grandmother's Montenegrin embroidered coat was the envy of everyone in school!

The hippies took it even further. Ethnic was in, which meant that long skirts, peasant blouses, babushkas, Gypsy earrings, beads, sandals, more beads, dashikis, caftans, and Indian *anything*—as long as it was cotton and tie-dyed— were very important.

On the dressier side, there appeared see-through fabrics which made body stockings necessary; jump suits; mammoth zippers on everything; belted tunics; patent vinyl skirts and vests; hot pants; and, as a real shocker after all those thigh-baring hemlines, maxis and midis.

Boys wore clothes with a distinctly Western flavor—lots of leather vests and blue work shirts—and took shelter from the elements in army jackets as a way of "doing a number" on the Establishment.

A colorful time when anything but anything went, the sixties were fashion mad. If you wanted to link plastic squares together with brass rings and call it a dress, well, far out! By contrast, the seventies were fashion happy. Trying so hard to be different and being so intense about it were tiring; the

Look what Tom Jones did for the unbuttoned shirt! *(1965)*
Martha K., Connecticut

I always thought calling them go-go boots was tacky. *(1967)*
Sherry A., New York

I used to wonder where they found those wild clothes. Guys even skied in red jackets with all the gold braid! *(1968)*
Beth C., Colorado

The cotton bandanna pulled low over the forehead and big gold hoops said it all for that time. *(1969)*
Carrie S., Arizona

I remember the looks I got when I first wore a midi coat—a lot of stares and what passed for disapproval. *(1969)*
Lea F., Pennsylvania

1940s

1948

1940s

Before and after.

1950s

whirlwind subsided into the calm after the storm.

Overnight the ubiquitous faded patchwork or patched jeans were crisply replaced by designer jeans in various shapes. Now they looked as if they could go anywhere—and they could!

Practical was *in*. Construction boots, flannel work shirts, denim purses, clogs, overalls, jump suits, and down vests assumed the status of uniform. The "can't miss" element in every wardrobe was the T-shirt—shaped, initialed, logoed, adorned, rainbow-hued. Casual ones bore messages that were simply fun—as opposed to heavy statement—and even these gave way to nonverbals like hearts and flowers and frogs on lily pads. Running a close second was the striped rugby shirt, another English import.

Hemlines, which had gone below the knee in 1970 with the much-criticized midi, stayed there. And even girls who never got out of pants got out for bigger and longer skirts to wear with all sorts of sweaters which in turn were accessorized with all manner of scarves. As skirts went fuller and swirlier, pants went straight; shapeless was bad news!

Boots hung in there, having joined the fashion pantheon for all time. Besides, they were a winter must. Teens in colder climates went to great lengths to keep warm and look good at the same time. Little knit hats, scarves, mittens, and leg warmers brightened up many a winter landscape—as did the later and incredibly popular down coat.

The seventies' obsession with physical fitness contributed tremendously to teen fashions. If one could own but one pair of shoes, let them be the running kind! The blue and gray sweat suits of old, which rarely left playing field or gym, turned up in all the best places and left their owners asking for more—which they promptly got in the form of warm-ups and jogging suits in every conceivable stripe and style. Out of boys' lockers came athletic shorts to quickly become an essential ingredient of a teen's dresser—of which at least one drawer might be reserved for high socks! As the enrollments in exercise and dance classes soared, the standard-issue leotard underwent all kinds of changes in style and fabric, and these too worked their way onto the street as shapely and relatively inexpensive tops—and the ideal complement to gym shorts.

Lots of eyes were on Texas by the late seventies when

My jeans were so tight, I had to lie down to squeeze into them. *(1972)*
Cathy K., District of Columbia

Remember those large belt buckles? Some had trucks, initials . . . whatever. Mine was a Coors buckle. *(1977)*
Paul K., New Jersey

Our legs froze, but it was far more important to wear a rabbit fur jacket than a long coat. *(1976)*
Candice W., New York

Wearing boots all the time meant you didn't have to worry about runs in tights or panty hose! *(1972)*
Betsy L., Massachusetts

So many kids wear running suits all the time that our town on a weekend looks like an Olympic village. *(1979)*
Kurt Z., New Jersey

1960

1950s

the urban cowboy strode into focus. Running shoes were heaped in a pile to make room for cowboy boots and intentionally baggy jeans shoved aside to accommodate Western shirts and straight-leg jeans. The eyes roved on and lighted upon the Southwest and its Indian heritage. Beaded moccasins, concha belts, squash blossom necklaces, and big silver and turquoise earrings did wonders for prairie skirts and miles of fringe.

If you wanted to ignore regional color, there was always the comfort of a denim skirt, a plain T-shirt, and rope-soled espadrilles.

Thrift shops were being scouted again, but this time for menswear of the Annie Hall variety. A touch of the baggy could be very charming. Across the country stores selling retro clothing did a land-office business in recycled uniforms, British officers' shorts, camouflage wear, Hawaiian shirts, and stewards' jackets.

Then it was time to look to England again, but some of the eyes turned to a nearer east—the East Coast of the United States and a style of clothing that had never been fashionable nor a fashion but simply indigenous: preppie! The race was on. Attics filled up as closets were cleared for khaki and corduroy and madras and neon-colored Shetland sweaters and pale Oxford button-downs and pastel Fair Isle sweaters and alligator shirts in every color in the spectrum and turtlenecks ascramble with strawberries and hearts and frogs. Knee socks returned with a vengeance for wear with what? Good old loafers! While the no-sock look won an A-plus for teens in boating mocs or duck shoes.

Those who preferred to throw caution to the winds liked what they saw in England and quickly brought it home: punk. It might mean something as quiet as "crucifying" a polo shirt by wearing a safety pin through the alligator, or it might be as noisy as the wearing of thirty pounds of unprecious metal (pins, studs, chains) could make an individual clank! Serious punk meant garish hair dyes—like bright green—bizarre makeup in shades ranging from black to ebony, startling hairdos for wearers whose heads made them look startled, and clothing that ran the gamut from clearly "retro" fifties to the outrageously harsh look of ripped everything!

Its successor, new wave, has taken some of the sting out of punk. Retro is the password, and plastic necklaces, Capri pants, pink flamingos, swizzle sticks topped with palm fronds, baggy jackets and pants, and fifties' hair for guys especially are getting lots of mileage.

I don't wear jeans anymore. I dress up more with designer corduroys and ruffled blouses. *(1983)   Alicia D., New Jersey*

By the eighties hemlines were on the rise again, and the summer of '82 saw lots of teens bare their legs in short, short skirts to the delight of all onlookers. It had been too long!

Designer jeans continue to hold their own, but the offerings are many. Just when you think there is not another thing that can be done to good old denim, stonewashing and dyes appear and the results are being grabbed up as quickly as the snug, above-the-ankle (or shorter) styles. Regular pants are freestyle; they can be snug as tights or jodhpurs, knickers, cropped, Zouave, whatever.

Right now, it's triple-pierced ears and Indian Earth makeup. *(1983)   Jackie Q., Indiana*

Boots have gone shorter to balance all the new shapes, and short boots (the kind Mother wore in the fifties) are finding favor everywhere, especially elf boots (last seen accompanying a pair of stretch slacks in 1962). Short skirts have caused yet another old favorite to be revived—the flat—and teens are learning how it feels *not* to have sore calf muscles.

There is romance in the air in the eighties, and it appears that ruffles and flourishes are here to stay for a while. Frilly blouses, slit or side-buttoned skirts, big belts, and dresses to unleash all sorts of fantasies are back on the racks. Teens are even eyeing basic black tuxes with interest—and not as anachronisms!

And they *are* spending a lot of time in the stores. The Valley Girls of Southern California, who certainly have sisters all over the map, love their malls and the constant shopping they afford, even if a day's search nets but a pair of feather earrings. What is fun, excellent even, is being dressed, turned out, lookin' *good*!

One could say it is all just bitchen, but they said that back in 1962, didn't they?

1930s

What fun is it being a teenager if you don't dress a little crazy? *(1983) Pamela S., Utah*

1950s

1950s

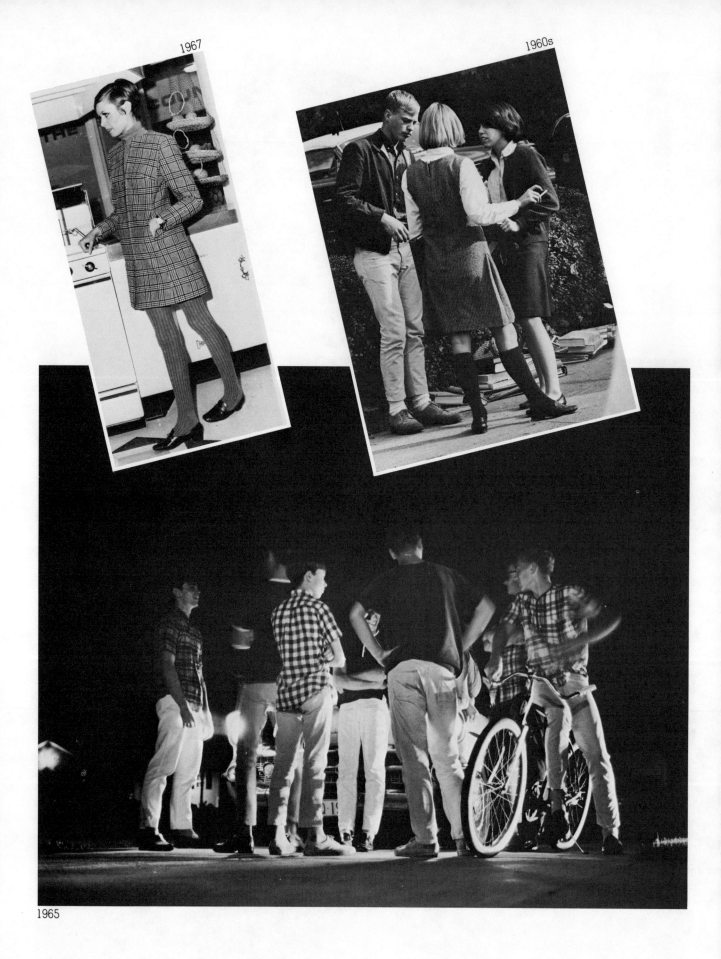

1967

1960s

1965

1978

1980s

1970s

1970s

7

Lend Me Your Comb

All I can remember about my hair is 'A little dab'll do ya.' Nice and smooth. *(1928)*

Eric M., Massachusetts

Hair. The long and short of it have made headlines, caused beelines—to barbershop, beauty parlor, and salon—and rivaled hemlines in the rise and fall department. And for teens, no battle cry ever rang so shrill as the parental, "If you *don't* brush that hair out of your face...!"

With gay abandon Flaming Youth broke rules and broke with tradition, so it was inevitable that the flappers would do away with those long tresses that had been considered a "woman's crowning glory" for hundreds of years. What they wanted and what they got was a snug little head to go with all those short little dresses. It was called a bob and it came in a wide assortment: orchid, coconut, moana, and boy.

Boys' haircuts of the twenties were remarkably uniform. Long hair was for artists and musicians, while beards were for Bolsheviks and bums! Accordingly, Joe College wore *his* neatly clipped, patent-leather hair parted down the middle. The daring types just might have their hair waved—but *only* their hairdressers would know for sure!

And then along came Rudolph Valentino, and proved a force too strong to resist. Thousands of teenage "sheiks" honored their idol and dazzled their best girls by sporting long sideburns and slicked back pompadours.

Short hair had gotten old by 1930, and teens were ready for longer locks again. Shoulder-length and smooth side-parted or with bangs, perhaps even permanented with lots of tiny little curls, hair grew as hemlines dropped. By 1936 there was an almost-anything-goes attitude: curls, loose waves, Indian-straight, a bare forehead, bangs, hair brushed behind ears—it was all acceptable *and* fashionable.

But it was the Depression. As fashion took a backseat to economy, teen boys only got a haircut when they badly needed one—or when they could find a classmate who would charge a dime. Yet there were some changes. The patent-leather look was passé, the pompadour was distinctly unfashionable, and hair was rarely parted in the center. It remained short, but now any natural wave was allowed to do its thing—sometimes even encouraged!

My graduation present was getting a boy-bob cut—I just loved it. *(1925)*
Emily C., New York

Sure hair was important. The boys' room was always filled with fellas fussing with their curls and parts. *(1930)*
Robert Y. Florida

I liked the boxed cut. Got it cut that way once—then there was trouble at home. *(1939)*
Patrick S., Pennsylvania

My father would dictate how I would wear my hair. He'd whisper something to the barber. Then I knew—short! *(1936)*
Jack G., Colorado

1920s

Different strokes.

1947

1958

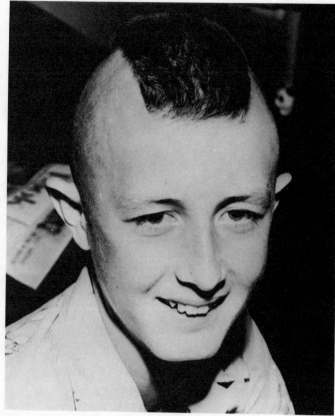

1952

A summertime haircut was always a crew cut—no questions asked. *(1945)*

George K., New Jersey

In the early forties, no teenage girls had to be encouraged to copy a hairstyle. There was only one that mattered, it came from Hollywood, and *everybody* wanted it: the Veronica Lake look. It was long; the hair fell straight from the top of the head for about eight inches before it began a gentle wave—right over the eye. It was utterly irresistible! Boys loved it, mothers cursed it, and moralists were truly alarmed. So much so, in fact, that they called the style the striptease, sheep dog, and bad girl. Nice girls couldn't get to their hairdressers fast enough!

Boys were not immune to the Hollywood influence, either. Their hairstyles were set by young film stars and entertainers. However, the only real change in the early forties was that wavy hair was not only acceptable but fashionable. A comb and a little water worked wonders for the straight-haired; and for those who insisted that straight was better, there was the bonus of good cuts which gave the hair fullness.

The year 1943 found teen girls eager for easy-to-manage

hair, which meant only one thing: it had to be short—preferably three inches all over, with soft waves and curls brushed loose.

No such length for their best guys, however. The GI cut was the big thing, and it allowed one and one-half inches max! Surprisingly, it did not fade away at the end of the war; the crew cut (or butch or flattop) remained the dominant style for some twenty years or more.

For those girls who had stayed with long hair, there was a route to a shorter *look*. This entailed moving it off the neck and to the top of the head in an upsweep that was called the doughnut, the sausage, or the topknot!

The late forties saw teens concentrate on somewhat shorter hair, but now it was important that the hair look lush and thick—and frame the face. The best style was the one that flattered you most, which probably meant it had big waves and soft curls.

The fifties ushered in a wagonload of possibilities for teenage girls. One-step coloring processes made experimentation hard to resist—and the results could make homeroom discussions very lively! Temporary coloring—the kind that washed out—created all sorts of fads, like streaking, and spraying your hair to match your clothes, and gold and silver sparkles for the big night out.

Boxes of bobby pins reposed on teens' dressers everywhere, all the better to secure pin curls with. Short, side-parted hair with curls over and in front of the ear scored high. Its big contender was the ponytail, a fifties trademark if ever there was one. What better accompaniment for the poodle skirt, bobby sox, and saddle shoes!

The styles came and went: pageboy, short and shaggy (courtesy of Italian movie stars), the D.A., also known as the duck tail and otherwise known as the first unisex hairdo, bouffant, headband- and bow-anchored poufs, butch cuts, pixies, and even an Elvis cut which transfixed teens in Grand Rapids, Michigan.

Boys stuck to their flattops, but Elvis proved an irresistible lure; besides, thousands upon thousands of girls were fainting at the sight of him! So, the boys grew their hair and their sideburns and cultivated a shock that worked its well-oiled way down the forehead.

The late fifties saw pin curls and bobby pins and metal

I used peroxide to streak my hair. Sometimes I'd even use hairglitter if I was going out on a date. *(1953)*
        Marcia R., Oklahoma

This sounds like punk, but I would match my hair color with dresses. I'd use a little hair rinse to go with my pink dress. *(1961)*
        Jeannie P., Illinois

The problem with the ponytail was the boys. For some reason they always yanked on it. *(1954)*
        Carol R., Florida

1970s

1950s

'TWIXT

Headsets.

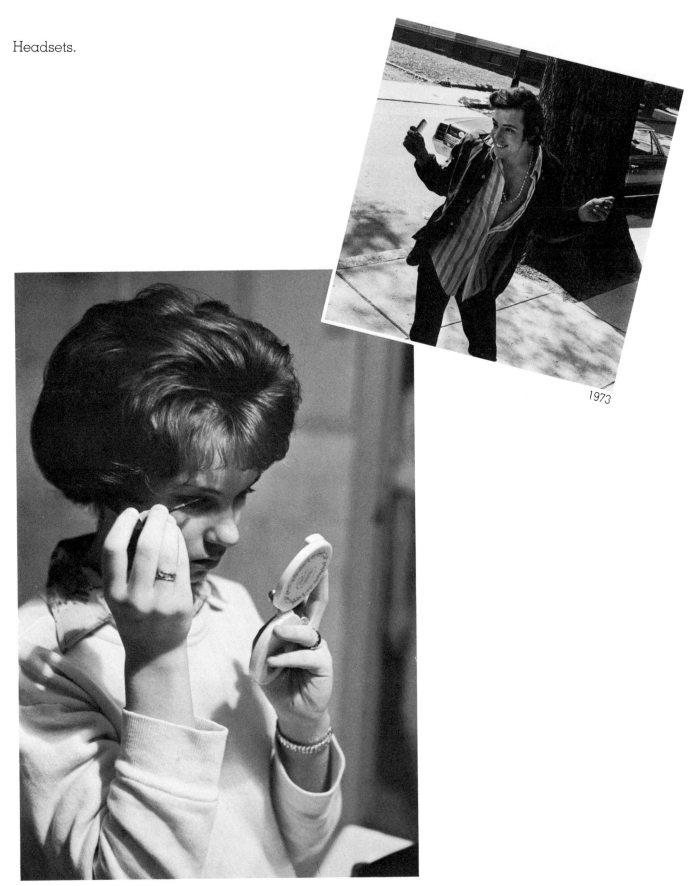

1973

1967

I used to go through jars of Vaseline because I'd put a glob in my hair to comb it down. *(1959)*

Peter J., Massachusetts

We all wanted to look like Sandra Dee or Connie Stevens. My hair was real puffy. It was called bubble hair. *(1962)*
Susan K., Texas

It wasn't easy getting a Beatle cut. First I had to let my hair really grow out. *(1964)*
Bob P., Wisconsin

clips rendered obsolete by a wire mesh or plastic device that plumped hair into bounce and fullness and nighttime agony. Ah, rollers, and heads wired for sound.

In the early sixties, a big sister of the fifties' bouffant took over. The beehive was adopted by teens immediately; the higher the better! Teasing was catapulted to high art, and hair-spray cans took their rightful place next to rollers and picks and nightcap. Artichoke, bubble, and flip bobbed through high-school corridors everywhere. And skulking through those same hallways were the tall stories about tall hairdos that made even the most secure of the wearers slightly nervous. (You know, like the one about the girl who didn't touch her beehive for months and months, just kept on spraying, until someone noticed blood trickling down her neck; when a doctor investigated, he found lots of little creepy-crawly visitors. No joshin'!) What were not so unbelievable were the complaints of classmates who couldn't see the teacher or of school authorities who were told beehived girls couldn't fit through the doors!

The boys kept a much lower profile. Short and very clean-cut hair was the most popular, not to mention a welcome departure from the crew cut. Modified greaser dos still *did* for a not insignificant number, however.

In 1964 came a very significant gust from England that would change everything. The Beatles arrived wearing what some called a modified fifteenth-century cut and what others labeled mop-top soup bowl. Whatever your comment, the hair looked long to Americans—especially since it covered the forehead. The furor was deafening—wearers were barred from class and commencement exercises—but the imitators were legion. And, if you dared not chance the cut, there were always Beatle wigs!

Another British import was playing to packed houses on Broadway, and it took about five minutes for the ragamuffin, Artful Dodger cut of *Oliver!* to make its way onto lots of pretty teen heads. The upkeep was a cinch.

What was not a cinch but what was certainly a longed-for look was the ubiquitous flip. Getting the ends to turn up just *so* taxed many a teen—and her hair-spray can. Rain was by far the worst enemy, for nothing looked so bedraggled as a droopy flip. (Of course, there were always those life-savers in the form of plastic rain hats that tied under the chin!)

Friday and Saturday nights at the dinner table usually proved to be otherworldly events for American families with teenage daughters. Bathrobe-clad girls arrived in puffy space bonnets (concealing an army of rollers) with dryer hose attached or disconnected as the wearer desired. Little pinch marks on the forehead were a dead giveaway later on.

It was therefore quite a happy day for many teens when Twiggy arrived direct from London with that short, geometric little cut that required a couple of rollers on top and artful use of cellophane tape otherwise.

Mods and rockers and go-go girls gave way to hippies and flower children and the counterculture. As these tightened their respective grips on the sixties, girls followed boys

1969

The D.A.—you know what *that* stands for! (1958) *Mark R., Illinois*

1962

1967

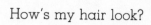

1965

1970s

and let their hair grow to lengths generally unseen but for Beatnik-inspired individuals. Teasing was out, but rollers the size of beer cans—and even empty juice and beer cans—were very much in. What was most important—and novel—was the freedom to let your hair go as you wished—despite what parents or school might say. All those folks with the truly curly hair—whom you might never have envied but who had probably envied you at least twice—were now in the vanguard. The longer and fuller (this latter was helped immensely by a head of natural curl), the groovier it was. Fat hair was far out. No more torturing the tresses with minds of their own with irons or straighteners, and no more

1970

1977

living in fear of humidity or rain; hair sprang free, and its owners basked in newfound glory.

With all that long hair around, it was becoming harder and harder to tell the girls from the boys, especially since they all went for the same accessories: rolled bandannas, feathers, beaded headbands, and earrings. Newspapers and magazines and parents got lots of mileage out of "Which one is the ———?" photos, but there were telltale beards and mustaches, which gave parents and schools something to wrestle with besides hemlines!

By 1968 there were all sorts of liberation afoot, and it turned the heads of young hair stylists across the country. Their young clients wanted great-looking haircuts—something akin to British rock stars—with no fuss. Wash and wear hair salons that catered to both sexes and bore clever names sprouted up everywhere, and thousands of hip stylists wielded blow dryers at the enormously popular shag cut. There wasn't a roller in sight, but the sounds were pure rock!

When that look ran out of steam, there was always short and smooth or long and smooth; here again, the blow dryer was essential, but so were heated rollers and curling irons. A little flipped-back curl at each side gave a nice fillip—and the impetus to go even further eventually, with lots of feathery curls around the face, as Farrah Fawcett inspired her thousands of teen admirers to do.

Curls *au naturel* were very popular, and permanents gave those who weren't born with them ample opportunity to enjoy a "now" look. If you were one of those who thought even a blow dryer represented too much effort, a perm was an answer to your prayers. And, wonder of wonders, boys tried it, too, and nobody minded or laughed. The freedom was intoxicating!

In 1976 a champion figure skater asked a top New York stylist to create something for her that would withstand the rigors of an Olympic performance and look smashing at the same time. Enter the Dorothy Hamill or wedge cut. It was an instant hit, and variations can still be found in 1983.

Long hair on young men lost its punch as the seventies wore on; anyway, it was no longer a statement. Everyone had it, even Dad! Where mustaches and beards had been part of all that, now they were tolerated, but the preference was for the well-trimmed variety. Clean-shaven was begin-

We took turns ironing each other's hair—hoping not to burn it. What an awful stench! *(1971)*
Audrey R., Ohio

My girlfriend and I had the same haircut. *(1970)*
Bruce H., California

I wasn't going to get a haircut—or get suspended. So I wore a short-haired wig to school. *(1972)*
Roddy T., Texas

I'm not embarrassed getting a permanent. I think it's excellent. I want curly hair, so... *(1983)*
Frank A., New York

Long hair meant protest, man. *(1967)*
Chris V., Connecticut

ning to look very new to lots of teens. As was shorter hair. Afros were trimmed close, straight hair was clipped to what had once been termed English schoolboy or Ivy League, and curls and waves were tamed. The new order, discipline, and conservatism of the Me Generation was clearly communicated by the hairstyles they chose to wear.

In 1979 gasps were heard in movie theaters across the country as a young and beautiful star-to-be named Bo Derek emerged on a beach, her blond hair in dozens of narrow braids studded with hundreds of tiny beads. Cornrowing, a hairstyle previously known only to blacks, swept teens off their feet, and thousands spent hours and lots of money getting creditable imitations. Its drawback, of course, was its execution and maintenance, which only meant that it was destined to spawn all sorts of attractive and less taxing variations.

It seems that braids are in for the long run; teens in the eighties wear the French braid and the numerous adaptations it affords.

Their nonconformist peers of both sexes opt for very short hair in the punk style and are not necessarily content to stop at a bizarre cut. Brilliant colors like red and yellow and purple and green light up their hair, which is often slicked into improbable shapes.

New wave has gentled punk somewhat, while taking much of its inspiration from the fifties. (It *was* about that time to look back again!) Boys take honors for the shortest styles.

These aren't the only retro looks. In 1982 rockabilly music reappeared and with it all the mid-fifties accouterments: pompadour, ponytail, and D.A.—albeit with some new twists. But by far the biggest surprise is the return of the fifties crew cut. Inspired in part by the haircuts of the film *An Officer and a Gentleman*, such tonsorial wonders as the Ivy League, Flattop Boogie, Marine Cut, Skinhead, Philly, Buzz, and Brush are lending variety (even a long curl or two) to the generally no-frills crew cut. It *is* the eighties, after all!

Just as those neon pink and green sweaters mingle with the flashback Hawaiian and geometric shirts in the high-school halls, so, too, do preppie hairstyles with punk, new wave, and rockabilly. It's strictly Ivy League for boys, and long, straight, maybe streaked or frosted, and headbanded for girls—which is to say that the more things change...

But we've heard all that before!

I grew a mustache so I would look older. It helped with girls and also I wouldn't get carded. *(1978)*
　　　　Alan H., Indiana

Punk hair, color and all, for sure. *(1982)*　　*Beth W., New Jersey*

I'll be looking for a job after graduation; I don't want my hair to blow it. *(1982)*
　　　　Jayne B., Florida

There are only two ways to go, layered or feathered. The boys like it, and that's all that counts, folks! *(1983)*　　*Susan T., Iowa*

1980s

1980

1960s

Crowning glories.

1981

1980s

'TWIXT

1980

1982

Eighties hair: punk, preppy, perm!

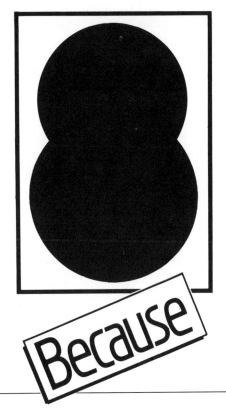

Because

I felt honored that our class sold enough war bonds to win us a citation. *(1944)*

Sandra M., Massachusetts

I think we can make changes through the right channels today and with the right attitude. *(1982)*

John G., Wisconsin

The visible symbols of the teen life-styles—dress, fads, music, dances—tend to loom so large as to obscure the many serious causes in which teens have participated over the decades. Though their protests have distinguished themselves with regard to time and place and kind, they all embody that essence of teen spirit which cuts across their generations: an energy of exceptional proportion.

There was little room for student radicalism in the twenties. Teens' protest ran to shocking the nation with their newfangled fads and fashions—not to mention their newfound freedom from authority. The fruits of their labors—the Charleston, drinking illegal hooch, flapper dresses, necking in parked cars, and the lure of college and all the temptations that lurked there—kept their minds fully occupied!

During the Great Depression, however, teen antics took a backseat to economics; *everyone* was expected to pitch in. Many students were forced to drop out of school and go to work. Some two and a half million young men joined the Civilian Conservation Corps. Supervised by the Forest Service and the army, CCC youth planted trees, treated tree diseases, dug ditches, built reservoirs, cleared campgrounds, and restored historic sites, for which they were paid $30 a month, most of which was sent home.

CCC and NYA (National Youth Administration) were the earliest and most popular youth programs of public service. They served as precedents for other such programs of the late sixties—Job Corps, Neighborhood Youth Corps, Peace Corps, Vista, and Youth Conservation Corps—and provided opportunities toward which young people could direct their energies and make some kind of contribution to society.

The mid-thirties saw college and high-school students shed their passive role and demand control over school activities. They joined organizations to protest war, poverty, and school policy. On April 13, 1934, twenty-five thousand participated in a national student strike against war. Two years later, three hundred and fifty thousand college students followed suit and joined a walkout.

It didn't take long for student protest to work its way into

I vividly remember the Depression. My father taught me to peel stamps off old letters. I still do it! (1933)   Perry S., Texas

My generation was politically apathetic. We had no time, except to look for work. (1932)   Jason V., New York

Students were very responsive. In fact, my brother took part in a one-day strike at Columbia University. It got pretty rough. (1932)   Pat J., Connecticut

'TWIXT

Top, Soothing striking highschool students in Camden, N.J., after a walkout to protest the transfer of six teachers; *middle*, Gloucester, N.J., highschool students support the strike for shorter hours in order that the football players might have more time to practice; *bottom*, thirty years later, New York City students strike for full rights.

1937

1935

1967

Left, Washington, D.C., students sell defense stamps for the war effort; *bottom*, North Carolina youth help save the crops, in response to the manpower shortage caused by WWII.

1942

1944

'TWIXT

the high school. In 1935, Gloucester, New Jersey, students walked out of classes in an attempt to persuade the superintendent of schools to shorten the school day—that football players might have more time to practice!

By 1937, even junior high schools were insisting on certain rights. Seven hundred students at a junior high school in New Jersey protested the transfer of six popular teachers by refusing to attend classes. They not only shouted down a Board of Education member but marched to the neighboring high school where they noisily attempted to gain support.

The war effort occupied forties' teens for the first half of the decade. Some worked in gas stations, on farms, and in factories while their fathers fought overseas. Others sold war stamps, collected wastepaper, and wrote letters to the troops. Still others enlisted. The war colored everything, and the talk in school centered on beating the enemy and winning.

The postwar years were not marked by protest beyond internal school problems, and these were decidedly minor, but the ground was at last fertile. While still observing traditional boundaries and not yet ready to take overt action, students contemplated the ills they perceived.

But the fifties brought yet another war, and this time high-school students demonstrated their support by writing letters and sending money to the troops in Korea. It wasn't to be so clear-cut and simple ever again.

The Supreme Court's 1954 decision to desegregate the country's schools fueled another kind of cause for some teenagers, and one which lasted well into the sixties. In Baltimore, thousands of white teens marched on City Hall to protest integration, while in New Orleans in 1960, thousands met outside the offices of the school board to protest integration of local schools. Later the police had to resort to fire hoses to clear the demonstrators from the streets. Clearly, teen protests had taken a startling turn.

On the other side of the issue, lots of sixties college students joined Southern blacks in the struggle for civil rights, aiding in demonstrations, legal battles, and voter registration drives. Though the tactics and philosophy were nonviolent, the opposition was not. Several teenage Freedom Riders were killed before it was all over.

In 1963 the assassination of a president much loved by the young drew students by the thousands to Washington,

The war was very much a part of teenage life. It was discussed everywhere—at home, at school—we were part of it. (1943)
Joe G., California

Many young fellas returned home in coffins. It was very sad and often affected the whole school or neighborhood. (1944)
Jeffrey B., Kentucky

My parents and I disagreed. I wanted to go, my parents said no. Hell, the GI was my hero...so I went. (1943)
William T., Louisiana

We couldn't express ourselves like today's youth. There were a few who spoke out, but many of us were still asleep. (1949)
Joan R., Iowa

D.C., for the funeral march. John Kennedy's interest and faith in youth had struck a very responsive chord in his young audience; he convinced them that youth was not only special but could make a difference.

> Let the word go forth... that the torch has been passed to a new generation of Americans—born in this country, tempered by war, disciplined by a hard and bitter peace, proud of our ancient heritage—and unwilling to witness or permit the slow undoing of those human rights to which this nation has always been committed...

The new generation of Americans listened very carefully,

1942

Above, San Francisco students collect scrap metal to aid the war effort; *top right*, remembering the boys in Korea: New York City students collect money to send to G.I.s; *bottom right*, Chicago students scorch scarfs with kisses for G.I.s.

fully, then plunged in. The civil rights issue had ignited the student movement, and the fires could not be extinguished. The flames licked on hungrily as demonstrations against the House Un-American Activities Committee, and the Free Speech Movement, were fueled, and then erupted into an unparalleled conflagration over the Vietnam War.

But the tragedies of the latter part of the decade were not confined solely to the Vietnam War. In 1968, the heir apparent, Robert F. Kennedy, who stood to inherit and perpetuate the Camelot that his older brother had so memorably created for America, was cut down five months before the presidential election; and Martin Luther King, Jr., the black

1952

1942

Baptist preacher who rose to become the eloquent teacher of a popular and effective political philosophy, succumbed to an assassin's bullet in Memphis. It seemed the dreams would never stop shattering.

The sixties had become the decade of student protest. Sit-ins, teach-ins, be-ins, marches, rallies, draft card burning, and even love-ins were regular as rain—but never as forgettable. Yet not all the fires were big nor fed by social conscience; dress regulations, student freedom, drinking, spring fever, whatever—the young found cause to revolt.

The "flower children" of the sixties were urged on by an endless supply of Pied Pipers to tune in, turn on, and drop out. Many took the advice straight to heart, others ignored it altogether. But whatever one's preference, the young didn't hesitate to come together when the opportunity arose—especially if it meant just *being* together with their music and its persuasive sentiments. The legendary concert at Woodstock drew three hundred thousand in 1969; four years later, six hundred thousand traveled to Watkins Glen, New York, for yet another festival.

The course of the student movement was not without nasty twists and turns, but in May 1970 the going got unbearably rough. At Kent State University in Ohio, a small detachment of a National Guard unit turned and fired upon rock-throwing students, killing four. That tragedy ended not only the movement but the decade.

The turnaround was nothing short of amazing. The earnestness remained, the desire to make a difference was firm, but the targets had changed. Environmental groups declared an Earth Day in 1970 to make people aware of the ecological problems confronting the nation. Young people everywhere cleaned, marched, and learned. In New Jersey hundreds of teenage volunteers helped clean the Hackensack River, while junior-high students marched through Kirkwood, Missouri, to protest the smog caused by automobile exhaust fumes. In Gorham, New Hampshire, teens cleared trash from the streets. Teach-ins, workshops, panel discussions, and debates survived into the seventies but focused on pollution, overpopulation, and the environment.

The mood mellowed steadily. As college campuses fell silent, the watchful eye shifted to the high schools but found only that high-school students were following in the quiet

I felt self-centered, but in a positive way. I was concerned with my health, the environment and a career. These were strong teenage ideals. *(1976)*
Fay M., New York

1967

1979

1963

Top, Joan Baez sings out in support of the blacks' struggle for equal rights during the 1963 march on Washington; bottom, high-school students go all out for McGovern in his bid for the presidency; opposite, a lone teenager strikes a note during the 1969 march on Washington to protest the Vietnam war.

1970

1969

footsteps of their older brothers and sisters. "Turning inward" was the operative phrase.

With years of crises, conflicts, turmoil, war, assassinations, riots, and demonstrations behind them, seventies' teens fastened on settling down, pursuing their own interests—and maybe even a few pleasures.

In 1972 the eighteen-year-old vote became a reality, enfranchising 11.1 million new voters. At long last the voice had been given to them, and many teens threw their weight behind peace candidates.

Teens of the late seventies and early eighties found interest in two popular issues—the draft and nuclear energy. Youthful demonstrators strongly protested against a 1980 law requiring the draft registration of all eighteen-year-olds. More than a half million young people across the country refused to sign up, arguing that registration was the first step in the process that could eventually lead to another Vietnam-style conflict.

Somewhat reminiscent of the flower children, thousands of teens joined in a series of nationwide demonstrations to protest nuclear energy. Rallies and blockades took place at the site of existing and proposed nuclear power facilities, including repeated marches at Seabrook, New Hampshire. In 1980 nearly two thousand gathered on that site during a Memorial Day protest. In June of 1982, scores of teens swelled the largest political demonstration in U.S. history. Three-quarters of a million people marched through the streets of New York City to Central Park where they listened to speakers such as Coretta Scott King and to such sixties-familiar singers as Joan Baez and Jackson Browne. Like the sixties protests in some ways, yet distinctly unlike them in others, this outpouring of sentiment was notable for its calm, its order, and its commitment to a peaceful show of hands.

As each generation discovers its own problems—the environment, war, injustice, morality, the economy—it seeks to find its own answers. The spirit of each generation has developed not only out of reaction to current issues but also out of concern with conditions for the future, political or social. Young people are often the visible conscience of society. They represent a spirit of change and hope; for this, many look upon them with gratitude.

Being able to vote was very important to me. I felt I counted and the politicians were paying attention. *(1976)*

Dan D., California

Sure we get involved today. The big issues are; Can I get to college? Can I afford it? Will I find a job? *(1983)*

Alan S., Massachusetts

1963

1970

Below, High school girls lead the march down
Fifth Avenue in New York City in support of
women's rights; *opposite top*, helping out with
sidewalk blood pressure tests; *below*, Buch-
anan, New York, youth protest the atomic power
plant at Indian Point.

1970

1970

1979

My Hero

Wow, we had them everywhere—the president, astronauts, movie stars, TV, and rock 'n' roll stars. So
many heroes! *(1962)*   *David H., Minnesota*

What's a hero? *(1983)*   *Jill T., New York*

Teenage heroes —their styles may change, but they never go out of style. Some jet into prominence, only to disappear like skywriting; others never fade away and are carried right along through life with us.

The twenties had more than its share of heroes, and Hollywood was a major source. Joan Crawford was the flapper *par excellence*; her screen antics in *Our Dancing Daughters*—kissing, drinking, dancing the Charlestown—were widely admired and imitated by teenage girls everywhere. Naughty was nice!

Heading the list of twenties' sex symbols was Clara Bow, Hollywood's glamorous "It" girl, who starred in the 1927 silent movie of the same pronoun. "It" was a quality of "strange magnetism" and "physical attraction," and popular opinion had it that Clara Bow had *it* all! At the age of twenty-one, the diminutive, big-eyed former beauty queen and flapper was a leading box-office draw. Alas, her sex appeal lasted only as long as the silent movies lasted—which was as long as she was able to hide from the public her heavy Brooklyn accent!

Her successors didn't have such problems. Alla Nazimova, Pola Negri, Gloria Swanson, Mae Murray, and Greta Garbo filled the list out nicely and gazed from the silver screen down onto audiences of teenage girls who yearned to look just like them.

Handsome Rudy Vallee was the twenties' crooner with a big following, but it was film star Rudolph Valentino who had an explosive impact on teens. Based on a 1921 novel by Edith Maude Hull, Valentino's film, *The Sheik*, established a romantic image that set all of young America gasping. Valentino played a millionaire Arab chieftain who carried off to his tent a beautiful, innocent girl who became his sexual slave before she fell in love with him. With the 1926 sequel, *The Son of the Sheik*, Valentino's popularity soared again—so much so that police were called upon to break up a mob of screaming women at the film's opening in New York City.

I wish I had a picture to show you—we all tried to look like Joan Crawford in those days. *(1928)   Agnes S., Massachusetts*

We used to say that Garbo was the bee's knees. *(1928)*
        Mary Jo M., California

Frank Sinatra, the King of Swoon, melting the hearts of bobbysoxers at New York's Paramount Theater.

1943

1943

1930s

1950s

'TWIXT

In the slang of the twenties, *sheik* meant a compelling and passionate lover of the Rudolph Valentino stripe!

When Valentino died of pleurisy in 1926 at the age of thirty-one, at least four women committed suicide. Fifty thousand mourners, many of them fighting each other for a view of the body, filed through the doors of the mortuary to pay last respects to their very own sheik.

Twenties' teens were known to look back—and toward Washington—for at least one hero. Although he had died in 1919, Theodore Roosevelt had earned himself a place in the hearts of the young. Not only had he charged into the twentieth century, he had been, at a reasonably tender age, a police chief, a natural scientist, an elected official, a rancher, a soldier, a war hero—and the twenty-sixth president of the United States. His White House rang with the sound of children, laughter, and frolic—just as it would some sixty years later when John F. Kennedy and family moved in.

Flaming Youth had a lot of time for sports, and they did love their Babe. Babe Ruth captivated his young fans, many of whom dreamed of playing in the major leagues and rising to the top as Babe had so magnificently done. His monument is Yankee Stadium, "the house that Ruth built."

The Babe's handsome contemporary, Charles Lindbergh, or the "Lone Eagle," flew the Atlantic solo in May of 1927 and instantly became a hero—not to mention making a lot of hearts soar! Youthful and daring, he was the quintessential all-American boy.

At twenty-five he was little more than a teenager himself, an unpretentious tousle-haired boy, who lived on sandwiches and chocolate bars. Teens responded to his feat by sending him millions of letters and packages and by starting fan clubs in schools across the country.

During the thirties, the need to escape the doom and gloom atmosphere of the Depression had teens flocking to films as never before to see the bigger-than-life song-and-dance team of Fred Astaire and Ginger Rogers, the blond bombshell Jean Harlow, James Cagney, Edward G. Robinson, James Stewart, and the traffic stopper himself, Clark Gable.

The most popular form of entertainment during the Depression era, however, was delivered by the forty million radios in American homes. Teens (and their parents) listened

Well, Valentino was big, sure. And lots of boys copied his hairstyle and ways—he was great. *(1927)*
James H., New York

I had great esteem for Teddy Roosevelt because he overcame many childhood difficulties. There's a man who went on to become a genuine hero. *(1925)*
Jeffrey T., New Mexico

There are several individuals I considered heroes and sought to imitate: Theodore Roosevelt, Charles Lindbergh, and my teachers." *(1928)*
Van B., Massachusetts

Opposite top, Benny Goodman, the King of Swing; *bottom*, fans letting go at a rock 'n' roll concert.

Well now, Jack Armstrong was a hero. He was just a character on radio of course, but he was the all-American boy. *(1936)*

Jack K., Indiana

I can recall playing outside and my father running to tell us President Roosevelt was going to speak on the radio. Suddenly the streets were empty. *(1934)*

Walt R., Kansas

I used to scream so hard for Sinatra that my throat would get sore. When I saw him in person in New York, I thought I was going to die. *(1942)*

Julie R., New York

Frank Sinatra was a snooty little cutie! *(1944)*

Margaret A., Illinois

to Bing Crosby and Kate Smith sing and to the comedy routines of Jack Benny, Burns & Allen, and Edgar Bergen and his dummy, Charlie McCarthy.

Weekends found young people gathered in hippodromes to listen to the music of their favorite swing musicians. Count Basie and Benny Goodman could do no wrong!

Not all of the heroes of the thirties came from show business. During the Depression's darkest days, teens were inspired by the programs and policies of Franklin Delano Roosevelt, the thirty-second president of the United States, who promised nothing less than to pull the country back onto the road to prosperity. To them, Roosevelt was a miracle worker, and he infused his young fans with hope.

In 1942 a scrawny-looking singer who stood only five feet ten inches and weighed 135 pounds was hardly considered a serious contender for idol status. Or so everyone thought. But Francis Albert Sinatra took the country by storm anyway and soon was known as the King of Swoon! His velvet voice melted the heart of bobbysoxers everywhere, and his appearance at the Paramount Theater in New York brought his fans to near riot. Hordes of them, clad in sweaters, skirts, white tennis socks, and saddle shoes, reached eagerly to touch him or tear a "souvenir" from his clothing. In 1944 more than twenty-five thousand teen admirers stormed the Paramount in Times Square and smashed box-office windows until police arrived to restore order and help Sinatra fight his way inside.

More than five hundred Sinatra fan clubs sprang into being in the forties and bore such names as "Slaves of Sinatra," "The Girls Who Would Lay Down Their Lives for Sinatra," and the "Society of Sinatra Swooners." Young Blue Eyes said it himself. "I'm twenty-five, but look like nineteen. Most kids feel like I'm one of them. They feel they know me, that's what I want. What the hell! They're nice kids!" In any event, the shy, sincere, vulnerable, and innocent teenager under that bravado came across, and he conquered all.

The serious hero of the forties was GI Joe—the boys in uniform who fought bravely around the world to defend America during World War II. Millions of teenagers had family members, neighbors and friends who were or soon would be soldiers—or WACS or WAVES or SPURS. They did not hesitate to rally behind the men and women in uniform and pledged their support through school programs, public demonstrations, and strong spirit. GI haircuts, field jackets, and combat boots were very popular, and teenage girls prepared packages for the boys over there and spent lots of time knitting their guys socks and scarves. They all followed daily radio and newspaper reports avidly and prayed for a safe return.

The GI Bill of Rights gave the World War II veterans an opportunity to go to college and accounted for swelled enrollments in the postwar years. These student veterans of the forties became the parents of the college students of the sixties. How differently the American GI would figure in *their* pantheon of heroes.

Frank Sinatra may have been the first teen hero to become a teen idol. Most certainly he was a star, a superstar before the term came into use. In 1956, however, even the word *star* was not big enough to describe accurately the man of the moment. Only *king* would do for the remarkable Elvis Presley. Rock 'n' roll created many stars, but none shone brighter than Elvis.

It all started with an appearance on the *Ed Sullivan Show*. Fifty-four million people tuned in, and Elvis immediately turned the teenagers' world upside down and inside out. The hazel-eyed, long-locked, sideburned, and swivel-hipped crooner twisted and writhed into the biggest idol teens had ever seen, and he would stay on top for *ten* years. Teen magazines and newspapers quickly got the message; *everyone* wanted a piece of the real Elvis!

His sexy dancing and "Come hither" voice earned him the title of Elvis the Pelvis. All across the country teens rushed to buy Elvis fashions and imitate that style; even the most conservative willingly let their crew cuts grow! And the girls— well, not since Sinatra had America seen anything like it. I want you, I need you, I love you ... Elvis!

Presley moved on into movies as Sinatra had before him. Films like *G.I. Blues* boosted his yearly income into the six-million-dollar category. And speaking of GI blues, millions of fans were shocked to learn that their main man was to be drafted in April of 1958. The king's crown was being forcibly traded for a GI cap. It didn't cramp his style in the least. The hits kept on coming: "Are You Lonesome Tonight?" "Love Me Tender," "A Big Hunk O' Love," "It's Now or Never," and many, many more.

Tyrone Power, he's my hero. I saw one of his movies five times! *(1947)   Midge R., California*

I still have my collection of Elvis pens, scarves, and autograph books. I keep them with my high-school yearbook and marriage certificate. *(1959)   Linda G., Missouri*

It took a lot of courage to give the order to drop the A-bomb. I admired President Harry Truman. That was an incredible decision to make. *(1945)   James K., New Jersey*

Eisenhower was the greatest. He provided the good life for us. Why do you think we had so much fun in the fifties? *(1954)   John F., Louisiana*

1960

1964

Left, The pied piper of the teenage set, Dick Clark; *right*, Boston fans go wild for the Dave Clark Five.

Elvis never faded away but toured the world with his hits, dazzling audiences everywhere. Twenty-one years and still a giant—until August of 1977 when a heart attack ended it all. The king was gone—never to be forgotten. The world mourned, and scores of teens—present and former—remembered, flooding his Graceland mansion in Memphis, some even collapsing at the sight of his coffin.

When rock 'n' roll burst into the mid-fifties, it sent shock waves in all directions, some of which were to affect profoundly the style of radio programming which in turn would forge an entirely new relationship between the music, the disc jockey, and the teen audience. The master of the Top 40—the deejay—was the crucial link. Teens rallied around popular radio personalities—"This is Dandy Dan Daniel in New York and we're the good guys"—who did not let them down. Disc jockeys were not only countin down the hits, they were hosting record hops and Saturday-night dances. They were celebrities, they were teens' heroes, and they were very often wild and zany: "This is your geater with the heater, your boss with the hot sauce," also known as Jerry Blavat in

Philadelphia. They *could* become as important as the music! Teens started fan clubs and rushed deejays for their picture and autograph when radio stations launched fun promotions with their newfound heroes. Girls excitedly entered contests to win a date with their favorite radio personality, while others baked cookies or sent their favorite deejay a pizza with "everything on it!"

The lineup of radio stars in each city swelled. Many were able to continue on past the peak of rock 'n' roll and move right into rock music. Alan Freed, Murray "The K" Kaufman, Ted Brown, Jocko Henderson, William B. Williams, Cousin Brucie Morrow, Dan Ingram and Don Imus all have lit up the New York scene. Los Angeles has had its share of sparks, too, in B. Mitchell Reed, Robert W. Morgan, and the Real Don Steele. They sold color and they sold boss radio, like Chicago's Dick Biondo, Howard Miller and Larry Lujack; Boston's Bob Clayton and Arnie "Woo-Woo" Ginsberg; Pittsburgh's Rege Cordic and Porky Chedwick; Cleveland's Bill Randle; St. Louis' Jack Carney; Detroit's Robin Semour; and San Francisco's Tom Donahue.

Syndicated radio personalities like Wolfman Jack, who appeared in the film *American Graffiti*, and Casey Kassem, who today counts down the national hits every week on radio stations all over the United States, have drawn large followings.

The mid-fifties also saw teens develop an interest in another medium—television—and its hit show, *American Bandstand*. Host Dick Clark was catapulted to the status of teen idol almost immediately. The popular teen dance show provided an absorbing and intimate experience to which Dick Clark's mild, easygoing personal style was perfectly suited. His manner was consistently relaxed, controlled, and quiet. His image was that of an attractive older brother or uncle. A distinguished personality who understood and sympathized with teens and enjoyed their music—but did not try to be one of them—Dick Clark took his place behind the music and let the dancing describe rock 'n' roll's vitality and impact.

And he *has* lasted. *American Bandstand* is still on the air, and Clark's television specials continue to draw big viewing audiences while generating that magic that places him within the pantheon of teen heroes. For his part, he looks younger than ever!

I love calling the DJ and talking and stuff...but their line is always so busy, busy, busy! *(1983)*   Sharon M., California

Let's hear it for Annette, Fabian, Frankie Avalon, and Spin and Marty. *(1959)*
     Eddie H., South Carolina

Dick Clark was Mr. Nice Guy. I think he should have become president. *(1960)*
     Sandra M., Nebraska

Yeh, yeh, yeh!

1966

1960s

'TWIXT
156

1981

1920

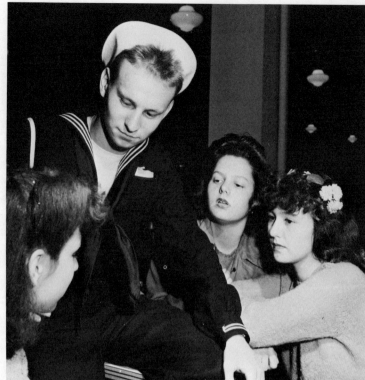

1943

Left, America's 'Lone Eagle, Charles Lindbergh; *right*, the teen hero of the forties—the G.I.

The first astronauts were heroes—Alan Shepard and John Glenn. They were like the Wright brothers. *(1961)*
Betty T., North Dakota

In 1960, when you left the television stage or turned off the set in the rec room after *Bandstand* and ventured outside, there were some who would tell you that you dwelt in Camelot. They had good reason.

When John F. Kennedy won the presidency, youth won, too. The decade of youth was at hand. JFK promised the future to the young, and he became their prince. The special feeling between Kennedy and young people was palpable; he became the best-loved hero since Elvis.

And then, in 1963, the most alarming news teens had ever heard crackled over P.A. systems everywhere: "The president has been shot." It would never be such a nice world again.

Assassination belonged in history books, not here, not to this president. His death left teens shocked and aching. Not since Lincoln's assassination had there been such national trauma as that caused by the death of Kennedy. Teens who had never even marched in a parade hurried to Washington for the funeral procession, to be there for their prince. The torch had been passed.

At the beginning of 1964, Americans still experienced a lingering gloom over the death of their president. The ground was right. Teens desperately needed to be captivated, and so they were—by that foursome from Liverpool, England, called the Beatles. The Beatles offered young people not only happiness and frivolity but their own youth—while generating more public enthusiasm and reaction than any individual or group in rock's history. They even topped Elvis' 1956 appearance!

Every album was greeted with the sort of anticipation and rush usually reserved for conquering heroes, and every visit or tour with the sort of frenzy associated with the bewitched! They made movies which came to be emblematic of the decade and which were seen again and again. And so it was, when the group decided to split up in 1970 to pursue their individual careers, that teens and postteens everywhere mourned. Yet the individual albums from John, Paul, Ringo, and George came steadily and with great success, and the fabulous four were simply never out of the public eye. Wild rumors of their reuniting for a tour or a concert spread like prairie fire at least once a year until, of course, December of 1980 when John Lennon, gifted composer, musician, and singer, and husband, and father, and genuinely adored ex-Beatle, was struck down by a bullet in front of his apartment building in New York City. John had been quiet in the last few years, turning from his music to other concerns, but now he was *back* and releasing albums with his wife, Yoko Ono; his fans were delirious. It therefore surprised no one that the outpouring of grief ran to candlelight vigils, moments of silence, and massive tributes. For those who had come of age in the sixties under the guiding light of the Beatles, losing John Lennon was something like losing a bit of yourself.

In 1956 an obscure young minister named Martin Luther King, Jr., rose to national prominence for his leadership of a 381-day bus strike in Montgomery, Alabama. When King's own home was bombed during the long siege, thousands of blacks threatened to riot, but the gentle King convinced them to throw their weight behind nonviolent protest—and thereupon became renowned as a champion of passive resistance. Within eight years, he became the acknowledged leader and most respected spokesman of America's blacks.

Young blacks and whites saw that sit-ins and lie-ins and

I went to an all-night vigil for John Lennon and held a candle in the cold air. Most of the people there shared the same feeling—that their own youth died with him. *(1980)*
Larry R., New Jersey

1930s

1960s

pray-ins were in fact powerful new weapons which were on their way to becoming the basis for a new heroic role in American life. And Martin Luther King gathered young people around him. He promised them a role in the future and asked for their participation and their courage. They gave both freely.

Martin Luther King's inspiration was felt in schools, on the streets, and in homes all over. He offered a new model, a new and better way, a peaceful road that would lead to freedom. His death, then, by an assassin's bullet cut deeply into the dream he preached and prayed for, but the young did not let go of what he had taught them.

> Free at last, free at last,
> Thank God Almighty, I'm free at last.

Robert Kennedy picked up where his brother left off. More than a junior senator from New York, Bobby became a folk hero, a new prince for youth under whom Camelot might once again flower.

He was youthful himself. It may have been the shaggy hair, the enthusiasm, and that contemporaneity derived from his empathy with the young. "I feel comfortable with young people," he said, "probably because they don't take me seriously or themselves seriously."

He addressed students everywhere, calling them the most idealistic and generous of all generations. And, oh, how they loved him for it. This was the decade when the entire world appeared to be against them. Everywhere he went he inspired youth, especially those who looked to him to fulfill his brother's plan. "You and I as young people have a special responsibility to carry on John's fight for a better future." Said one senator of Bobby, "He had the future written all over him."

But the future would never be his. Yet another assassin's bullet took Bobby, and young America mourned again, the third time in five years. Our flowers had all gone.

Bob Dylan has been called "Poet Laureate of the Flower Children." Many claim he was the first poet of the mass media. Whatever your feeling, there is no disputing that his 1962 recording of "Blowin' in the Wind" became the rallying anthem for young people's involvement in the protest movement.

The Kennedys inspired me. I cried when JFK was shot. When we lost Robert, I felt it was all over for young people's dreams. *(1968)*   *Kenneth W., Indiana*

Neil Armstrong. I stayed up late to see him walk on the moon. Next day I stuck a picture of him on the back of my bike. *(1969)*
Chad G., Pennsylvania

Dylan's sandpapery voice was the messenger for the young's complaints about the world they had inherited. By 1964 his songs were helping a whole generation get political, reflecting as they did a social awareness that could not be ignored. The freewheelin' Bob Dylan sang what everyone was feeling: "The Times They are A-Changin'."

It has been suggested—only half in jest—that teenagers of the late seventies and early eighties have no heroes, unless you are willing to count Pac-Man and Miss Piggy.

It is entirely possible that the Vietnam War; the assassinations of John Kennedy, Martin Luther King, Jr., Robert Kennedy, and John Lennon; repeated energy crises and economic recessions; attempted assassinations of Pope John Paul II and President Ronald Reagan; the Watergate scandals; and the untimely deaths of such young favorites as Jim Morrison, Janis Joplin, Elvis Presley, and John Belushi have had that sort of cumulative, defeating effect.

Mass media, especially TV, have greatly increased the visibility and status of the celebrity. The lines between hero, artist, and superstar have merged. Superstars pop up with each new season, hit record, movie, or popular TV commercial. Not surprisingly, today's teens claim superstars have replaced traditional heroes. So, while heroes appear to be having a bad time of it, superstars seem to thrive in this climate, and teens are devoting lots of attention to them.

Diana, Princess of Wales, and Britannia's brightest star, has captured the eye and the interest of America's teens. Diana is that thoroughly modern pincess who may just wander through the royal apartments wearing headphones and chewing gum to the beat of the Beatles. Youthful, sophisticated, endearing, capable, and very influential, she is a big hit with teens.

Two of America's top models, Brooke Shields and Cheryl Tiegs, are riding the wave of superstardom creditably. Dazzling their audiences from the covers of *Vogue*, *Mademoiselle*, and *Tiger Beat* with that remarkable glow, the success of both signals that the all-American girl image is in the ascendancy again.

A teenager herself, Brooke has attracted all sorts of attention to her roles as a teen in the movies *The Blue Lagoon* and *Endless Love*, and the forthcoming *Sahara*, *while* making no end of headlines about which college she'll attend

Say what you want, Gerald Ford made a big difference at a difficult time. *(1975)*
Barbara A., Arizona

I think we have the wrong kind of heroes today. Those people who try and shoot the president, or commit some strange crime, become media heroes. It doesn't make any sense to me. *(1982)*
Leo C., Arkansas

Princess Di is tops. I saw her story on TV and read about her, too. She's very classy. *(1982)*
Ellen D., North Carolina

1960

1957

1980s

Top, the rebel's rebel, James Dean; *bottom*,
the eighties comic without peer, Eddie Murphy.

and who she's dating. An especially committed teenager,
Brooke speaks out for antialcoholism and antismoking cam-
paigns.

From down under has come Olivia Newton-John, the
smashing Australian singer who likes to get physical! Her
performance as Sandy in the hit movie *Grease* with John
Travolta boosted her superstar image with American teens.
She's the one they love, ooh-hoo-hoo!

The list of teens' superstars in the eighties include several
personalities from the sports world. Middleweight champion

Sugar Ray Leonard is admired for his courage and character after being forced to end his boxing career due to an eye condition. His cool manner and easy style have earned him teenagers' respect.

Another championship fighter, Muhammad Ali, continues to draw praise from the young. Ali, who captured world attention for his repeated comebacks, gets high points for his honesty, discipline, and tell-it-like-it-is personality. Amen!

Score a home run for teen angel, Reggie Jackson. The powerful Los Angeles outfielder—often colorful and sometimes controversial—is a big hit with today's teens, who are rooting for his success with his new team.

And teenagers continue to root for the success of tennis superstar Chris Evert Lloyd. On the courts, they agree that Chrissie plays hard, fair, and with grace. Off the courts, teens add, the U.S. Open Champion is "real and the way we want our stars to be." That's a definite advantage!

My favorite subject is, Soaps 101! (1983) Andrea F., New York

And there's another group of superstars that teens can easily plug into: "The Boss," Bruce Springsteen; Billy Joel; Rick Springfield; Paul McCartney; The Rolling Stones; The Clash; The Police; and the Bee Gees.

Saturday Night Live…a great place to take a date. (1981) Jack R., Pennsylvania

Lastly, a very special category deserves very special mention: Most Admired. It will surely come as a surprise that eighties' teens place parents and friends at the top of the list.

Teens credit parents with greater degrees of openness and trust, enabling both to share feelings, hopes, problems, and dreams. Honest, forthright discussions have no bounds—they frequently revolve around each other's strengths *and* weaknesses—and result in a big plus: a mutual admiration society!

Friendships have always been a large part of the teen years; being able to confide in someone your own age is important—and comforting. The eighties have made all of that even better. Not only are closer friendships being nurtured, but boy-girl relationships that have nothing to do with dating are thriving. Such camaraderie is irresistible and healthy, and eighties' teens no doubt will be the richer for it.

So, there are heroes and there are heroes. We've seen that reports of the disappearance of the hero have been exaggerated. After all

Existence would be intolerable if we were never to dream.
Anatole France

1924

1982

1982

Opposite, *top left*, The 'It' girl, Clara Bow; *top right*, Lady Diana, Princess of Wales; *bottom*, Brooke Shields launching cosmetology classes for multi-handicapped persons; *this page*, *top*, Chris Evert Lloyd in fine form; *bottom*, Sugar Ray Leonard getting a helping hand from his son, Ray.

1976

1981

And When We All Got Together

Remember the times you'd invite one friend to come over? Next thing you knew, twenty kids showed up, and it was a party! *(1958)*   Judie M., Kansas

1920s

1951

1950s

1970s

'TWIXT

1941

1981

1961

1950s

'TWIXT

1980

1968

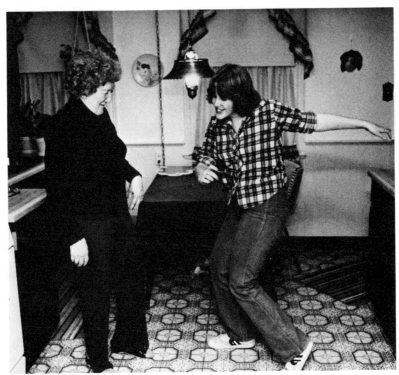

1981

And the beat goes on...